Transformed *for* Life

How to Know God Better and Love Him More

DEREK PRINCE

Chosen
Grand Rapids, Michigan

Published by Chosen Books
a division of Baker Publishing Group
P.O. Box 6287, Grand Rapids, MI 49516-6287
www.chosenbooks.com

Second printing, March 2005

Printed in the United States of America

Library of Congress Cataloging-in-Publication Data
Prince, Derek.
    Transformed for life : how to know God better and love Him more /
Derek Prince.
        p.   cm.
    Includes bibliographical references and index.
    ISBN 0-8007-9307-2 (pbk.)
        1. Spiritual life—Christianity. I. Title.
BV4501.3 .P76 2002
248.4—dc21   2002001413

CONTENTS

PREFACE

SINCE MY CONVERSION some sixty years ago, I have pursued the practical application of truth both for myself and my fellow believers. I was trained at the highest levels of perhaps the best educational system of its time, Britain. Much of my training was in esoteric and theoretical areas, however, having little application to everyday living. I have found that God's truth, by contrast, is very down to earth and practical. In fact, if something is not simple, I am usually somewhat suspicious of it!

The messages compiled in this volume are some of the most life-changing and practical that God has given me. Together they represent a powerful look at the transforming power of God as Father, Deliverer and Healer. The theme of transformation always brings to mind Romans 12:2: "Do not be conformed to this world, but be transformed by the renewing of your mind, so that you may prove what the will of God is, that which is good and acceptable and perfect" (NASB). I know of nothing more powerful than a transformed mind that is enabled to lay hold of God's perfect will!

I offer this book with the sincere prayer that multitudes will be transformed and conformed into the image of Jesus (see Romans 8:29).

PART 1

EXTRAVAGANT LOVE

EXTRAVAGANT LOVE. It will bring you into a new dimension in appreciating God and responding to Him. Does the word *extravagant* surprise you? It is appropriate because it refers, first and foremost, to the love of God.

The very nature of God is love. God is so much bigger and greater than we can imagine, and this is true of His love as well. Our human love is often petty, stingy and self-centered, but God's love is vast, boundless, extravagant!

This is a prayer Paul prayed for God's people in Ephesians 3:14–19:

> For this reason I kneel before the Father, from whom his whole family in heaven and on earth derives its name. I pray that out of his glorious riches he may strengthen you with power through his Spirit in your inner being, so that Christ may dwell in your hearts through faith. And I pray that you, being rooted and established in love, may have power, together with all the saints, to grasp how wide and long and high and deep is the love of Christ, and to know

this love that surpasses knowledge—that you may be filled to the measure of all the fullness of God.

NIV

The central theme of Paul's prayer for us: that we may know God's love. But we cannot make room for Christ to dwell in our hearts until we are strengthened with power by the Spirit. Paul prayed that we may be established in His love and that we may be able to grasp how wide, how long, how high and how deep it is. Then he concluded by praying that we might "know this love that surpasses knowledge. . . ." This is a paradox. How can we know love that surpasses knowledge?

I believe there is an answer: We do not know it with our intellect but through the revelation of Scripture and of the Holy Spirit. It is a revelation that comes to our spirits rather than to our minds.

The purpose of this section is to share with you various passages of Scripture that provide us with standards by which to measure God's love.

one

THE TREASURE IN THE FIELD

THE FIRST PASSAGE that provides us with a standard by which we can measure God's love is the story found in Matthew 13:44. It is Jesus' parable of the treasure hidden in the field.

A parable is a simple story about familiar, material, earthly things. The objects in Jesus' parables were familiar to all His hearers. But the purpose of a parable is to reveal unseen, eternal and spiritual things. The familiar scene and the familiar story then become a mirror reflecting unseen, unfamiliar, spiritual things.

Jesus proceeds in the method of a good teacher, moving from the known to the unknown. He starts with items with which His hearers are familiar and leads them on to those that are not familiar. As we read a parable, then, we need to ask ourselves, What are the spiritual things that correspond to the material things in the parable?

Let's look at this parable. Then I will give you my interpretation.

"The kingdom of heaven is like treasure hidden in a field. When a man found it, he hid it again, and then in his joy went and sold all he had and bought that field."

NIV

What are the spiritual realities that this simple story reveals to us? I am not suggesting that there are no other interpretations, but according to my view (which is in line with the principles of Scripture), the man who found the treasure is Jesus. The field is the world. (This image runs through the seven parables found in this chapter, and it is stated in Matthew 13:38.) What about the treasure? It is God's people in the world.

When the man discovered treasure in the field, he did something very wise: He did not immediately tell everybody. In fact, Scripture says he hid it. He knew that if people learned there was treasure in the field, there would be a lot of competition, so he hid the treasure again and decided to purchase the field.

Bear in mind that he really did not want the whole field; all he wanted was the treasure. But he was realistic enough to know that in order to get the treasure, he had to pay the price for the entire field. The price of the field for that man was high; it cost him all he had. But he did it with joy because he knew the value of the treasure.

Can you picture the surprise of the local residents? "Whatever does he want that field for? It's not really good for anything. It has little market value. It's not good for crops. All it produces is thorns and thistles. Why would he pay so much money for a field like that?" They did not know, you see, about the treasure. The only person who knew about the treasure was the man himself, who is Jesus. So He paid the price for the field (which is the whole world) in order to obtain the treasure that is in the field (which is God's people).

Let's look at another very familiar verse:

"God so loved the world that he gave his one and only Son [Jesus], that whoever believes in him shall not perish but have eternal life."

John 3:16, NIV

God loved the world and gave the life of His Son to redeem it. But what God receives out of the world is the *whoever:* "*whoever* believes in him shall not perish." That total company of *whoevers* is the treasure in the field that Jesus died to purchase. He redeemed the world for the sake of the *whoever.*

In Titus 2:14 we find the same truth. Paul speaks about Jesus Christ, "who gave himself for us to redeem us [buy us back] from all wickedness and to purify for himself a people that are his very own, eager to do what is good" (NIV).

There is that treasure again—a people who are His very own and who have been redeemed from the world, redeemed from wickedness, purified and made zealous to do what is good. The price was Jesus Himself—all He had, all He was. He laid down His life. He gave Himself to buy that field for the sake of the treasure, His redeemed people.

Let me offer one further thought about this treasure in the field. Jesus has bought the field, but He leaves it to His servants, the ministers of the Gospel, to recover the treasure. There is a lot of work involved. You must find where the treasure is, dig it up and take it out of the earth. It has lain there a long time and it is rusty, dirty, mildewed and corroded. It needs a lot of cleaning up. Again, Jesus does not do this work Himself. He has His servants in this world dig out His treasure with hard labor and clean it up.

Believe me, preaching the Gospel to people and bringing them to the Lord *is* hard work—just as hard as digging a treasure out of a field. But this is left to the ministers of the Gospel in this world, of whom I am one. The purpose: to get that treasure out of the field, clean it up and make it fit for the Lord. This is what Paul said about his own ministry:

We proclaim him, admonishing and teaching everyone with all wisdom, so that we may present everyone perfect in Christ. To this end I labor, struggling with all his energy, which so powerfully works in me.

Colossians 1:28–29, NIV

13

The whole purpose of ministry, according to Paul, is to proclaim the Person of Jesus. Paul was not content with leaving any of God's people below the level of their potential. He worked hard. Look at all the words that denote activity in these verses: *labor, struggling, his energy, powerfully works in me.* What is the purpose and direction of all that activity? To get the treasure out of the field, to get it cleaned up and to make it fit to present to the Lord, who died and bought the field with His own life. How do we proclaim Him? Paul says, "We admonish, we teach." His aim was to present everybody just as good as he or she can be in Christ.

But I want to remind you of the price that Jesus paid for the field and for the treasure that is in the field. The price was *all He had.* He held nothing back. His love was extravagant. And He did it with joy because He had such love for the treasure—for you and me.

two

THE PEARL OF GREAT VALUE

EVERYTHING ABOUT GOD is greater and grander than we can comprehend, but this is particularly true of His love. The very nature of God is love. The word I have chosen to describe this love is *extravagant,* an unusual and non-religious word, to get away from stereotypes.

Our human love is often petty, stingy and self-centered. God's love is not like that at all. It is vast, boundless and extravagant. Remember the prayer Paul prayed for all of us in Ephesians 3:

> For this reason I kneel before the Father, from whom his whole family in heaven and on earth derives its name. I pray that out of his glorious riches he may strengthen you with power through his Spirit in your inner being, so that Christ may dwell in your hearts through faith.
>
> verses 14–17, NIV

To comprehend what God has for us, we must first be strengthened by His Spirit. Something must be created in us as a receptacle for what He wants to put into us. Paul goes on to explain what that is:

> I pray that you, being rooted and established in love, may have power, together with all the saints, to grasp how wide and long and high and deep is the love of Christ, and to know this love that surpasses knowledge—that you may be filled to the measure of all the fullness of God.
>
> verses 17–19, NIV

God wants to put the fullness of His love into the vessel that He creates in us by His Holy Spirit. He wants us to know all the dimensions of His love—how wide, long, high and deep it is. He wants us to know a love that passes knowledge. God's love cannot be known by the intellect, but it can be apprehended through the revelation of the Scripture and of the Holy Spirit.

The parable of the Treasure in the Field, which we looked at in the last chapter, was used as a standard by which to measure God's love. It reveals the measure of Christ's love for His people *collectively.* Remember, buying the treasure cost Him all He had.

The parable that immediately follows, the Pearl of Great Value, reveals the measure of Christ's love for each human soul *individually.* It is important for us to appreciate that God loves us not just as part of a group but as individuals.

> "Again, the kingdom of heaven is like a merchant looking for fine pearls. When he found one of great value, he went away and sold everything he had and bought it."
>
> Matthew 13:45–46, NIV

In line with the previous parable, the merchant is Jesus. He was not just a tourist or window-shopper but someone who really knew the value of that for which He was looking. When He found this one pearl, He realized it would be a bargain to sell all He had just to buy it.

How many of us would see a stone so precious that we would part with everything we had just to own that one jewel? That is the love of Jesus. It is extravagant!

The cost of the pearl is the same as the cost of the field: all He had. (In the next chapter we will analyze what it meant for Jesus to give all He had.)

What does a pearl suggest? One thing it suggests in Scripture is suffering. A pearl is caused by irritation within the oyster. It is the product of something going wrong inside the shell. Isn't it interesting that all the gateways to the New Jerusalem are made of pearls? That tells us there is no way into the New Jerusalem except the way of suffering.

Then, in the process of making that pearl marketable, many things must be done. The pearl has to be raised from the depths of the sea, removed from the oyster and subjected to various processes. It is rather like the treasure in the field. It takes a lot of work to make it ready. Just as Jesus bought the field but leaves it to His servants to prepare the treasure for Him, likewise, He leaves it to His servants to ready the pearl for His enjoyment. But finally there comes forth that smooth, beautiful, gleaming pearl.

Picture Jesus holding just one pearl in His hand, looking down at it with inexpressible love. This is not a collective picture, not meant for a group, but something personal and individual. It is. Imagine Jesus with just one pearl gleaming in the palm of His hand, saying to that pearl, "It was for you I paid that price. I gave all I had."

Go one step further. Say to yourself, "*I* was that pearl. I *am* that pearl. If there had been nobody else to be redeemed, Jesus would have died just for me." It is important that you see this. Many of us struggle with a sense of unworthiness, inadequacy and rejection. We wonder whether we are really wanted. It is vital to see that each of us is a pearl for which Jesus gave all He had.

Here are four simple but very important facts about God's love:

God's love is individual.
God's love is everlasting.
God's love is from before time.
God's love is irresistible.

Let's look at some Scriptures that illustrate these four points.

God's love is individual and everlasting.

The LORD hath appeared of old unto me, saying, Yea, I have
loved thee [individually and personally] with an everlasting
love: therefore with loving-kindness have I drawn thee.
                                        Jeremiah 31:3, KJV

God's love is of old, both individual and everlasting. It is
out of His love that He draws us to Himself.

God's love precedes time.

For he [God] chose us in him [Christ] before the creation of
the world to be holy and blameless in his sight. In love he predestined us to be adopted as his sons through Jesus Christ. . . .
                                        Ephesians 1:4–5, NIV

There are two possible ways of punctuating this verse: "to
be holy and blameless in his sight in love . . ." or "to be holy
and blameless in his sight. In love he predestined us. . . ."
Whichever you use, the fact remains that God's love precedes
time. Before the creation of the world He loved us, chose us
and predestined us. He arranged the course of His life so that
we would encounter Him and encounter His love.

God's love is irresistible.

A simple statement in the Song of Solomon says, "Love is
as strong as death" (8:6). Death is irresistible. When death
comes, nobody can turn it away or say, "I'm not ready. I won't

accept you." No man has the power to resist death. And Solomon says, "Love is as strong as death."

The New Testament takes us one step further. When Jesus died and rose from the dead, He proved that love is stronger than death. The most irresistible, negative force in the universe was conquered by the most irresistible, positive force in the universe: the love of God. An old English song sung many years ago called "Love Will Find a Way" illustrates this:

> Over the mountains
> Under the fountains
> Love will find a way.

Love always gets to its objectives. It accepts no barriers. And the love of God will go through anything, over anything, under anything to get where it wants.

Think about that! God's love is *individual, everlasting, from before time* and *irresistible*. Then picture yourself again as the pearl in the hand of Jesus. Say to yourself, "His love for me is individual and everlasting. It precedes time. It is irresistible." Then remember what it cost Him—all He had. Stop to say, "Thank You."

three

Jesus Paid the Full Price

We have looked at two parables that give us a standard by which to measure what it cost Jesus to redeem us: the parables of the Treasure in the Field and the Pearl of Great Price. In each case the buyer had to sell all he had to make the purchase. This was true of Jesus. To redeem us cost Him everything.

Exactly what did it mean for Jesus to give His life on our behalf? First, the price of redemption was His own blood:

> . . . Knowing that you were not redeemed with perishable things like silver or gold from your futile way of life inherited from your forefathers, but with precious blood, as of a lamb unblemished and spotless, the blood of Christ.
>
> 1 Peter 1:18–19, NASB

Only by the blood of Christ could we be redeemed from our sins, our foolishness and our darkness. Why did it have to be by blood? The Old Testament gives the clear answer. The life, or soul, of all flesh is in the blood. If a living creature has a soul and has blood, then the life, or soul, of that creature is in its blood. This is stated in Leviticus 17:11, where Moses was given laws for living according to the principles of God:

> "The life [or soul] of the flesh is in the blood, and I have given it to you on the altar to make atonement for your souls; for it is the blood by reason of the life [or soul] that makes atonement."
>
> NASB

The blood atonement that took place in the Old Covenant was prophetic of the blood of Jesus given on the altar of the cross to make full and final atonement for our souls.

Bear in mind that the Hebrew word translated "life" is the Hebrew word for "soul." The *soul* of all flesh is in the blood of that creature. Isaiah prophesied that the Suffering Servant would give His life blood, and thus His soul, for us as atonement. Speaking prophetically about Jesus in that great preview of the atonement, Isaiah says that "he hath poured out his soul unto death: and he was numbered with the transgressors; and he bare the sin of many, and made intercession for the transgressors" (Isaiah 53:12, KJV).

Notice four statements about what Jesus did: He poured out His soul unto death; He was numbered with the transgressors (remember, He was crucified between two thieves); He bore the sin of many (actually, the sin of the whole world); and He made intercession for the transgressors (praying, before He died, "Father, forgive them, for they do not know what they are doing" (Luke 23:34, NIV). Every one of these statements was exactly fulfilled in Jesus.

But we want to focus on the first statement in verse 12: "He hath poured out his soul [or life] unto death." In order to get a clearer prediction of exactly what was to take place, we need to look at a passage in Leviticus.

The most important day in the religious year of the Jewish people was the Day of Atonement, known today as Yom

Kippur. On that day alone, the High Priest went into the Holy of Holies with the blood of the sacrifices that would cover the sins of Israel for one more year. This is how Moses described it:

> "He [the High Priest] shall take some of the blood of the bull and sprinkle it with his finger on the mercy seat on the east side; also in front of the mercy seat he shall sprinkle some of the blood with his finger seven times."
>
> Leviticus 16:14, NASB

The blood alone could propitiate the sins of God's people, and the blood had to be brought right into the presence of almighty God in the Holy of Holies. Notice particularly that it was sprinkled seven times. This was no accident. Seven is the number that indicates the work of the Holy Spirit. It is also the number of completeness or perfection. Seven indicates a perfect work that has been done.

As we look at the historical record of the gospels, we find the exact fulfillment of the Old Testament prophecies and types. The sprinkling of the blood seven times from Leviticus 16 was fulfilled exactly in the way Jesus shed His blood. In what ways was His blood sprinkled seven times before the sacrifice was complete?

The first sprinkling (or shedding) of His blood took place in the Garden of Gethsemane as Jesus wrestled in agony to make Himself available to God for this last great sacrifice.

> Being in anguish, he prayed more earnestly, and his sweat was like drops of blood falling to the ground.
>
> Luke 22:44, NIV

His blood began literally to come out of His body in His sweat. This was the expression of His agony and His wrestling, the first shedding of His blood.

The second shedding took place when He was in the house of the High Priest, being questioned and mistreated.

Then they spat in His face and beat Him with their fists; and others slapped Him.

Matthew 26:67, NASB

The word translated "beat Him with their fists" can also mean "beat with rods." This is probably more accurate because it was prophesied in Micah 5:1: "They will strike Israel's ruler on the cheek with a rod" (NIV). However it happened, the Lord was beaten with fists or with rods and blood came out of His face (probably out of His nose, among other places).

The third shedding of blood is recorded in Matthew 27:26:

Then [Pilate] released Barabbas to them. But he had Jesus flogged, and handed him over to be crucified.

NIV

This, too, was predicted in the Old Testament, where the Lord is speaking:

I offered my back to those who beat me,
     my cheeks to those who pulled out my beard;
I did not hide my face
     from mocking and spitting.

Isaiah 50:6, NIV

It is important to notice that the Lord *offered* His back. He was not compelled, but gave Himself as a sacrifice. He was flogged with a Roman scourge, which was made of many thongs, each one studded with bone or metal. When it fell across a man's back, it literally plowed his back and ripped up the flesh, exposing the sinews and even the bones. This was the third shedding of blood.

The fourth is not stated in so many words in the New Covenant, but we read it in Isaiah 50:6. Once again:

I offered my back to those who beat me,
     my cheeks to those who pulled out my beard. . . .

NIV

23

They took the beard of Jesus and pulled it out in tufts and handfuls, thus again shedding His blood.

The fifth shedding of blood was by the crown of thorns:

They [Roman soldiers] stripped him and put a scarlet robe on him, and then twisted together a crown of thorns and set it on his head.

Matthew 27:28–29, NIV

Actually, they did not just set it on His head. Those brutal soldiers, having woven the thorns (which you can see everywhere in the land of Israel today), pressed it down on His head and then beat Him on His head. This pressed those sharp thorns into His scalp—the fifth shedding of blood.

The sixth shedding of blood was the actual crucifixion:

When they had crucified him, they divided up his clothes by casting lots.

Matthew 27:35, NIV

His hands and feet were pierced with nails. This, too, was predicted in the Old Testament: "They have pierced my hands and my feet" (Psalm 22:16, NIV). And in verse 18: "They divide my garments among them and cast lots for my clothing" (NIV).

There remains the seventh and final shedding of blood, which took place after Jesus had died. A Roman soldier was sent to make sure the three persons on the crosses were dead. He killed the first two, but when he came to Jesus he saw that He was already dead:

One of the soldiers pierced Jesus' side with a spear, bringing a sudden flow of blood and water.

John 19:34, NIV

In that sevenfold shedding, the Lord's body was emptied of blood. He literally poured out His soul to death. He shed His blood seven times:

1. His sweat became blood.
2. They struck Him in the face with fists and rods.
3. They flogged Him with a Roman scourge.
4. His beard was pulled out.
5. Thorns were pressed into His scalp.
6. His hands and His feet were pierced with nails.
7. His side was pierced with a spear.

Remember, as you read this list, that it is the measure of His love, the price that He paid. It cost Jesus literally all that He had. He did not simply give up His glory, His throne and His majesty as God. He did not simply give up His few earthly possessions as a Man on earth. He gave up Himself, His own life. He poured it out in His blood as the price of redemption.

Think about that and realize the price that is the measure of God's love. To say the least, it is extravagant.

four

⁂

THE TOTAL INHERITANCE

WE WILL NOW CONSIDER what we receive in Christ through redemption: our limitless inheritance. Not only was God extravagant in the price He paid to redeem us, but He is equally extravagant in all that He gives us in Christ.

In Romans 8:15–17 Paul is telling Christians what is available to them through their faith in Christ.

> You did not receive a spirit that makes you a slave again to fear, but you received the Spirit of sonship. And by him [the Holy Spirit] we cry, "*Abba,* Father." The Spirit himself testifies with our spirit that we are God's children. Now if we are children, then we are heirs—heirs of God and co-heirs with Christ, if indeed we share in his sufferings in order that we may also share in his glory.
>
> NIV

The word *Abba* is Aramaic or Hebrew and corresponds to the English word *Daddy.* We enjoy a relationship of intimacy with God the Father whereby we address Him as *Abba,* "Daddy." The Spirit of God Himself gives us this confidence.

The Bible tells us we are God's children, but the Spirit of God reinforces that truth personally to each of our hearts: *We are God's children.* As normally happens in the human race, when we become children, we become heirs. As God's children we are made heirs of God and co-heirs with Christ. One condition is stated: If we share the inheritance, we must be willing to share Jesus' sufferings. Remember that the pearl is the product of suffering.

It is important to understand what it means to be co-heirs. It does not mean we each get a small fraction of the total inheritance. It means that since Jesus, as the first Son, gets the whole inheritance, we share the whole inheritance with Him. The law of God's Kingdom is sharing. We do not each grab our portion; we share together all that God the Father has and all that Christ the Son has. Each of us has a right, therefore, to the entire inheritance, which is the inheritance of Jesus.

Here is what Jesus, speaking about the coming of the Holy Spirit, says about this inheritance and how we can know about it:

> "When he, the Spirit of truth, comes, he will guide you into all truth. . . . He will bring glory to me by taking from what is mine and making it known to you. All that belongs to the Father is mine."
>
> John 16:13–15, NIV

All that belongs to the Father belongs to the Son. And the Holy Spirit, without whom we could not grasp this truth, will reveal to us all that it means. Remember, the Holy Spirit is the administrator of the inheritance. If we are not in a good relationship with Him, not walking in fellowship with Him, then we can be, in theory, children of the King but living like paupers and beggars because we are not entering into our inheritance.

The inheritance includes all that God the Father has and all that God the Son has. They share together and we share with them. This is the fullness of what God has bestowed on us in Christ. He is not stingy, not petty, not legalistic. He is extravagant!

Another Scripture speaks about the extent of our inheritance:

> He who did not spare His own Son, but delivered Him over for us all, how will He not also with Him freely give us all things?
>
> Romans 8:32, NASB

Consider the implication of these words. When we receive Christ, God freely gives us *all things*. Apart from Him we receive nothing. What a tremendous emphasis on the scope of the inheritance and on its absolute freedom! We cannot earn it. We receive it as a free gift, and it includes all things. When we receive Christ, then, we are heirs of the total inheritance—all that God the Father has and all that God the Son has.

Paul tries to show the Corinthian believers, who have been acting mean and petty and jealous with one another, how rich they are, and he rebukes them for acting as though they were poor. He says, in effect, "You people don't realize what you've got."

> So then let no one boast in men. For all things belong to you, whether Paul or Apollos or Cephas or the world or life or death or things present or things to come; all things belong to you, and you belong to Christ; and Christ belongs to God.
>
> 1 Corinthians 3:21–23, NASB

Isn't this a breathtaking statement? Paul is saying, "All things belong to you. Stop acting in a petty way. And don't get hung up with preachers, either. Stop being so small-minded. Everything is yours!"

Remember, all is given to us freely; we cannot earn it. But it is important that we ask the Holy Spirit to enlarge our faith and understanding. Unless He as the administrator speaks to us and guides us into the truth, these will be just words, not reality. It is the Holy Spirit who makes the promises a reality.

Finally we will look at two different translations of 1 John 4:16:

> We have come to know and have believed the love which God has for us. God is love, and the one who abides in love abides in God, and God abides in him.
>
> NASB

> We know and rely on the love God has for us. God is love. Whoever lives in love lives in God, and God in him.
>
> NIV

Notice the opening phrase, *We have come to know and have believed the love which God has for us,* and the alternative translation, *So we know and rely on the love God has for us.* There are two aspects. One is *knowing* the love God has for you, and the other is *believing* or *relying on* the love God has for you.

Many Christians hear Scriptures in church about the love of God. They may entertain them or even believe them. But these Scriptures do not become real until we *rely* on them. We must take seriously that God loves us and that He paid the highest price in the universe to redeem us. Once having redeemed us, He has made the whole inheritance ours.

We must begin to rely on that truth and to act on it. We must stop being mean, petty and stingy with other people (and with ourselves!), and learn to be like God—extravagant.

five

RETURNING EXTRAVAGANT LOVE

WE HAVE SEEN that the love of God for humanity can be measured by certain objective standards. First, it can be measured by the price that God and Jesus paid. That price is indicated in the two parables given in chapters 1 and 2 of this book: Jesus paid *all He had*. He poured out His soul, or His life, unto death (as we saw in chapter 3) in a sevenfold shedding of His blood.

Second, God's love for us can be measured by the inheritance He gives us in Christ. We are heirs of God and co-heirs with Christ. The entire inheritance of God the Father and God the Son becomes ours together with Jesus Christ. The tremendous scope of God's love can be measured by the price He paid and by the inheritance He offers.

We now want to look at the other side of the coin: How should we respond to God's extravagant love? Quite simply, we should be extravagant, too.

Let's look at the account of what one woman did for Jesus about a week before His death:

While he was in Bethany, reclining at the table in the home of a man known as Simon the Leper, a woman came with an alabaster jar of very expensive perfume, made of pure nard. She broke the jar and poured the perfume on his head.

Some of those present were saying indignantly to one another, "Why this waste of perfume? It could have been sold for more than a year's wages and the money given to the poor." And they rebuked her harshly.

"Leave her alone," said Jesus. "Why are you bothering her? She has done a beautiful thing to me. The poor you will always have with you, and you can help them any time you want. But you will not always have me. She did what she could. She poured perfume on my body beforehand to prepare for my burial. I tell you the truth, wherever the gospel is preached throughout the world, what she has done will also be told, in memory of her."

Mark 14:3–9, NIV

Jesus ends with a tremendous statement: "What she has done will also be told, in memory of her."

A parallel account in the gospel of John identifies the woman and brings out some other aspects of what took place:

Mary took about a pint of pure nard, an expensive perfume; she poured it on Jesus' feet and wiped his feet with her hair. And the house was filled with the fragrance of the perfume.

But one of his disciples, Judas Iscariot, who was later to betray him, objected, "Why wasn't this perfume sold and the money given to the poor? It was worth a year's wages." He did not say this because he cared about the poor but because he was a thief; as keeper of the money bag, he used to help himself to what was put into it.

John 12:3–6, NIV

Consider three important elements in this story: first, what Mary did; second, what Jesus said; and third, how the critics reacted.

What Mary Did

First, look at what Mary did. She was extravagant. She poured out ointment worth more than a year's wages. By contemporary standards in the United States, she poured out a pint of ointment worth at least $15,000 that was contained in a beautiful alabaster jar, which she also broke. The jar could never be used again. It was gone in just a few moments. That was extravagant!

Second, look at Mary's devotion. She not only poured the ointment on His head, as we read in Mark, but she poured it on His feet and wiped His feet with her hair, as we read in John. Picture the woman kneeling before Him, letting her long hair hang down, wiping the ointment on His feet and rubbing it in. Isn't that extravagant?

What Jesus Said

Now consider a number of powerful things Jesus said about this woman. He certainly did not side with the critics! He said of Mary, "She has done a beautiful thing to me" (Mark 14:6). We can be grateful for that translation. In her act Jesus saw something that struck Him as beautiful. Extravagant love *is* beautiful.

In verse 8 Jesus also said, "She did what she could." This is simple but important. God never asks us to do more than we can. We often hear people say, "I wish I could do more." But something in me always asks, *I wonder if they are really doing what they can?* God will never require of you more than you can do. But if you do what you can, the attitude of Jesus will be just the same as it was toward that woman.

Also in verse 8: "She poured perfume on my body beforehand to prepare for my burial." That is an amazing statement. None of the disciples really believed that Jesus was going to die at that time and be buried. Yet Mary, of all Jesus' followers, had the revelation that He *was* to die and be buried.

When He actually did die on the cross, His followers did not have time to anoint His body properly. They wrapped it in sheets and put some perfume and spices on it, but they could not do the real anointing; they had missed the opportunity. Mary was open to the Holy Spirit. He had spoken to her heart, not just to her head. There is a saying in the French language that originated with Pascal: "The heart has its reasons of which reason knows nothing." I think the heart of that woman had some reasons that all the people who sat and thought things through simply did not understand.

The tremendous reward of Mary is recorded in Mark 14:9. Jesus said that "wherever the gospel is preached throughout the world, what she has done will also be told, in memory of her" (NIV).

Even the message you are now reading is fulfilling that prophecy! It is just one fulfillment out of many.

How the Critics Reacted

First the critics were stingy, as religious people often are. Consider the phrase *poor as a church mouse.* That phrase is an awful giveaway! The world views church mice as poorer than other mice, and the Church as a poor, stingy group of people. A lot of Christians give them good reason to think that way! In this case, however, it was the critics who were stingy, not Jesus or Mary.

Second, those critics were hypocrites. They suddenly got concerned about the poor when they saw the ointment being poured out. We may question whether they had been doing much for the poor up to that moment, and whether they did much for the poor from that moment on.

Third—and this is typical of critics—they were miserable. They did not even enjoy the perfume. The whole house was filled with a beautiful fragrance, but they were so busy being angry and critical that they could not even enjoy it.

As we close part 1 of this book on the extravagant love of God, I want to ask you a personal question: Has the Holy Spirit ever touched your heart to be extravagant in your devotion to Jesus? You cannot do anything directly for Jesus Himself, because He is in heaven. But, like Mary, you can do something for His Body—His people on earth.

Consider the many remote areas of the earth—China, India, parts of Africa, Central and South America, the islands of the sea, parts of Europe and Asia. Many of the people who live in these areas, perhaps most of them, are, by American standards, extremely poor. They probably have no sheets on their beds. In fact, many of them probably do not even have beds. They may sleep on mats in huts. Many have no shoes on their feet. Most probably have no choice of food to eat. We are used to wondering whether we will eat this or that; we scarcely realize that the world is filled with people who never have that choice. Some do not have any food at all.

If you decide to try to reach these people, you are doing something for Christ's Body on earth. If the Holy Spirit touches your heart, will you be like Mary and dare to be extravagant? Will you dare to do something out of the ordinary? Religious people may criticize, but, remember, Jesus will praise you!

PART 2

THE DIVINE
EXCHANGE

JESUS CHRIST HAS GIVEN an invitation that extends to the whole human race: "Come to me, all you who are weary and burdened, and I will give you rest" (Matthew 11:28, NIV). No matter what your special burden or need or problem, God has an answer for you.

But there is only one place you can find the answer: the cross on which Jesus died. It is through the cross, and the cross alone, that you may receive the release from your burden, the supply of your need, the answer to your problem.

Read the following pages expectantly!

six

〇

What Is the Divine Exchange?

THE ENTIRE MESSAGE of the Gospel revolves around one unique historical event: the sacrificial death of Jesus on the cross. The writer of Hebrews explains that "by one offering He has perfected forever those who are being sanctified" (Hebrews 10:14, NKJV here and throughout Part 2). Two powerful words are combined: *perfected* and *forever.* Together they depict a sacrifice that meets every need of the entire human race. Furthermore, its effects extend throughout time and on into eternity.

It is on the basis of this sacrifice that Paul writes in Philippians 4:19, "My God shall supply *all your need* according to His riches in glory by Christ Jesus." *All your need* covers every area of your life—your body, soul, mind and emotions, as well as your material and financial need. Nothing is either so large or so small that it is excluded from God's provision.

Nor has God provided many different solutions for the multitudinous problems of mankind. Instead He offers us one all-sufficient solution, which is His answer to every problem. By a single, sovereign act, God brought together all the needs and all the suffering of humanity in one climactic moment of time. We may come from many different backgrounds, each of us burdened with our own special need, but to receive God's solution we must all make our way to the same place: the cross of Jesus Christ.

The most complete account of what was accomplished at the cross was given through the prophet Isaiah seven hundred years before it actually took place. In Isaiah 52–53 the prophet depicts a "servant" of the Lord whose soul was to be offered to God as an offering for sin. The writers of the New Testament are unanimous in identifying this unnamed servant as Jesus. The divine purpose accomplished by His sacrifice is summed up in Isaiah 53:6:

> All we like sheep have gone astray;
> We have turned, every one, to his own way;
> And the LORD has laid on Him the iniquity of us all.

Here is the universal problem of all humanity: We have turned, each of us, to our own way. There are specific sins that many of us have never committed, such as murder, adultery or theft. But this one thing we all have in common: We have turned to our own way. In so doing *we have turned our backs on God.* The Hebrew word that sums this up is *avon,* here translated "iniquity." Perhaps the closest equivalent in contemporary English would be *rebellion*—not against man but against God.

No one English word, however, whether it is *sin* or *iniquity* or *rebellion,* conveys the full meaning of *avon.* In its biblical use *avon* describes not merely iniquity but also the punishment, or evil consequences, that iniquity brings in its train. In Genesis 4:13, for instance, after God pronounced judgment on Cain for the murder of his brother, Cain exclaimed,

"My punishment is greater than I can bear!" The word here translated "punishment" is *avon*. It covered not merely Cain's "iniquity," but also the "punishment" it brought on him.

In Leviticus 16:22, concerning the scapegoat released on the Day of Atonement, the Lord said, "The goat shall bear on itself all their iniquities to an uninhabited land." In this symbolism the goat bore not only the iniquities of the Israelites, but all the *consequences* of their iniquities.

In Lamentations 4 *avon* occurs twice with the same meaning: In verse 6 it is translated: "The *punishment of the iniquity* of the daughter of my people" (verse 6) and in verse 22: "The *punishment of your iniquity . . .* O daughter of Zion." In each case the single word *avon* is translated by a complete phrase, "the punishment of iniquity." In its fullest sense, in other words, *avon* means not simply "iniquity" but all the evil consequences that God's judgment brings on iniquity.

This applies to the sacrifice of Jesus on the cross. Jesus Himself was not guilty of any sin. In Isaiah 53:9 the prophet says, "He had done no violence, nor was any deceit in His mouth." But in verse 6 he says, "The LORD has laid on Him the iniquity *[avon]* of us all." Not only was Jesus identified with our iniquity, but He endured all the evil consequences of that iniquity. Like the scapegoat that prefigured Him, He carried them away so that they might never return on us.

Here is the true meaning and purpose of the cross. On it a divinely ordained exchange took place. First Jesus endured in our place all the evil consequences that were due by divine justice to our iniquity. Now, in exchange, God offers us all the good that was due to the sinless obedience of Jesus. Stated more briefly, *the evil due to us came on Jesus, that in return the good due to Jesus might be offered to us.*

God is able to offer this to us without compromising His own eternal justice because Jesus has already endured on our behalf all the just punishment due to us on account of our iniquities.

All this proceeds solely out of the unfathomable grace of God, and it is received solely by faith. There is no logical explanation in terms of cause and effect. None of us has ever done anything to deserve such an offer, nor can any of us ever do anything to earn it.

What do we receive in the divine exchange?

seven

∞

ASPECTS OF THE EXCHANGE

SCRIPTURE REVEALS MANY different aspects of the exchange and many different areas in which it applies. In each case the same principle holds good: *The evil came on Jesus that the corresponding good might be offered to us.*

We Receive Forgiveness and Healing

The first two aspects of the exchange are revealed in Isaiah 53:4–5:

> Surely He has borne our griefs [literally, sicknesses]
> And carried our sorrows [literally, pains];
> Yet we esteemed Him stricken,

Smitten by God, and afflicted.
But He was wounded for our transgressions,
He was bruised for our iniquities;
The chastisement [punishment] for our peace was upon Him,
And by His stripes [wounds] we are healed.

Two truths are here interwoven. The application of one is spiritual, the other physical. On the spiritual plane Jesus received the punishment due us on account of our transgressions and iniquities so that we, in turn, might be forgiven and have peace with God (see Romans 5:1). On the physical plane Jesus bore our sicknesses and pains so that we, through His wounds, might be healed.

The physical application of the exchange is confirmed in two passages of the New Testament. The gospel writer Matthew, referring to Isaiah 53:4, records that Jesus "healed all who were sick, that it might be fulfilled which was spoken by Isaiah the prophet, saying: 'He Himself took our infirmities and bore our sicknesses'" (Matthew 8:16–17). The apostle Peter, referring to Isaiah 53:5–6, says that Jesus "bore our sins in His own body on the tree, that we, having died to sins, might live for righteousness—by whose stripes you were healed" (1 Peter 2:24).

The twofold exchange described in the above verses may be summed up as follows:

Jesus was punished that we might be forgiven.
Jesus was wounded that we might be healed.

We Receive Righteousness

A third aspect of the exchange is revealed in Isaiah 53:10, which states that the Lord made the soul of Jesus "an offering for sin." This must be understood in light of the Mosaic ordinances for various forms of sin offerings. The person who had sinned was required to bring his sacrificial offering—a sheep, goat, bull or some other animal—to the priest. After he confessed his sin over the offering, the priest would symbolically transfer the sin he had confessed from the person to the animal. Then the animal would be killed, thus paying the penalty for the sin that had been transferred to it.

All this was designed in the foreknowledge of God to foreshadow what was to be accomplished by the final, all-sufficient sacrifice of Jesus. On the cross the sin of the whole world was transferred to the soul of God's Son. The outcome is described in Isaiah 53:12: "He poured out His soul unto death." By His sacrificial, substitutionary death, Jesus made atonement for the sin of the whole human race.

In 2 Corinthians 5:21 Paul refers to Isaiah 53:10 and, at the same time, presents the positive aspect of the exchange:

He [God] made Him [Jesus] who knew no sin to be sin for us, that we might become the righteousness of God in Him.

Paul does not speak here about any kind of righteousness that we can achieve by our own efforts, but about God's righteousness—one that has never known sin. None of us can ever earn this. It is as high above our own righteousness as heaven is above earth, and it can be received solely by faith. This third aspect of the exchange may be summed up as follows:

Jesus was made sin with our sinfulness that we might be made righteous with His righteousness.

We Receive Life

The next aspect of the exchange is a logical outworking of the previous one. The entire Bible, both Old and New Testaments, emphasizes that the final outcome of sin is death. In Ezekiel 18:4 the Lord states, "The soul who sins shall die." In

James 1:15 the apostle says, "Sin, when it is full-grown, brings forth death." When Jesus became identified with our sin, it was inevitable that He should also experience the death that is the outcome of sin.

Confirming this, the writer of Hebrews 2:9 says that Jesus "was made a little lower than the angels, for the suffering of death . . . that He, by the grace of God, might taste death for everyone." The death Jesus died was the inevitable outcome of human sin that He took on Himself. He bore the sin of all of us, and so died the death due all of us.

In return, to all who accept His substitutionary sacrifice Jesus now offers the gift of eternal life. In Romans 6:23 Paul sets the two alternatives side by side: "The wages [or just reward] of sin is death, but the [unearned] gift of God is eternal life in Christ Jesus our Lord."

Thus the fourth aspect of the exchange may be summed up as follows:

Jesus died our death that we might receive His life.

We Receive Abundance

A further aspect of the exchange is stated by Paul in 2 Corinthians 8:9:

You know the grace of our Lord Jesus Christ, that though He was rich, yet for your sakes He became poor, that you through His poverty might become rich.

The exchange is clear: from poverty to riches. Jesus became poor that we in turn might become rich.

When did Jesus become poor? Some people picture Him as poor throughout His earthly ministry, but this is not accurate. He Himself did not carry a lot of cash, but at no time did He lack anything He needed. When He sent His disciples out on their own, they likewise lacked nothing (see Luke 22:35). So, far from being poor, He and His disciples made a regular practice of giving to the poor (see John 12:4–8; 13:29).

True, Jesus' methods of obtaining money were sometimes unconventional, but money has the same value, whether withdrawn from a bank or from the mouth of a fish (see Matthew 17:27)! His methods of providing food were also at times unconventional, but a man who can provide a substantial meal for five thousand men, plus women and children (see Matthew 14:15–21), would not be considered poor by normal standards!

Actually, throughout His earthly ministry Jesus exactly exemplified "abundance," as defined in the Bible. He always had all that He needed in order to do the will of God in His own life; and, over and above this, He was continually giving out to others, never exhausting His supply.

So when did Jesus become poor for our sakes? The answer is, *On the cross.* In Deuteronomy 28:48 Moses summed up absolute poverty in four expressions: *hunger, thirst, nakedness* and *need of all things.* Jesus experienced this in its fullness on the cross.

> He was *hungry.* He had not eaten for nearly 24 hours.
>
> He was *thirsty.* One of His last utterances was, "I thirst!" (John 19:28).
>
> He was *naked.* The soldiers had taken all His clothes from Him (John 19:23).
>
> He was *in need of all things.* He no longer owned anything whatever. After His death He was buried in a borrowed robe and in a borrowed tomb (Luke 23:50–53). Thus Jesus, exactly and completely, endured *absolute poverty* for our sakes.

In 2 Corinthians 9:8 Paul presents more fully the positive side of the exchange:

45

God is able to make all grace abound toward you, that you, always having all sufficiency in all things, have an abundance for every good work.

Paul is careful to emphasize that the only basis for this exchange is God's *grace*. It can never be earned; it can only be received by faith.

Very often our "abundance" will be like that of Jesus while He was on earth. We shall not carry large amounts of cash or have large deposits in a bank. But from day to day we shall have enough for our own needs and something left over for the needs of others.

One important reason for this level of provision is indicated by the words of Jesus quoted in Acts 20:35: "It is more blessed to give than to receive." God's purpose is that all His children be able to enjoy the greater blessing. He provides us, therefore, with enough to cover our own needs and also to give to others.

This fifth aspect of the exchange may be summed up:

Jesus endured our poverty that we might share His abundance.

We Receive Glory and Acceptance

The exchange at the cross also covers the emotional forms of suffering that follow from man's iniquity. Here again Jesus endured the evil that we in turn might enjoy the good. Two of the cruelest wounds brought on us by our iniquity are *shame* and *rejection*. Both these came on Jesus on the cross.

Shame can vary in intensity from acute embarrassment to a cringing sense of unworthiness that cuts a person off from meaningful fellowship either with God or with other people. One of the commonest causes (becoming more and more prevalent in our contemporary society) is some form of sexual abuse or molestation in childhood. Often this leaves scars that can be healed only by the grace of God.

The writer of Hebrews, speaking of Jesus on the cross, says that He "endured the cross, *despising the shame*" (Hebrews 12:2). Execution on a cross was the most shameful of all forms of death, reserved for the lowest class of criminal. The person to be executed was stripped of all his clothing and exposed naked to the gaze of passersby, who jeered and mocked. This was the degree of shame God's Son endured as He hung on the cross (Matthew 27:35–44).

In place of the shame that Jesus bore, God means to bring those who trust in Him to share His eternal glory: "It was fitting for Him [God] . . . *in bringing many sons to glory,* to make the author of their salvation [that is, Jesus] perfect through sufferings" (Hebrews 2:10). The shame that Jesus endured on the cross has opened the way for all who trust in Him to be released from their own shame. Not only that, but He shares with us the glory that belongs to Him by eternal right!

There is another wound that is often even more agonizing than shame. It is *rejection.* Usually this stems from some form of broken relationship. In its earliest form it is caused by parents who reject their own children. This rejection may be active, expressed in harsh ways, or it may be a failure to show love and acceptance. If a pregnant woman harbors negative feelings toward the infant in her womb, the child will probably be born with a sense of rejection—which may continue into adulthood and even to the grave.

The breakup of a marriage is another frequent cause of rejection. This is vividly pictured in the words of the Lord in Isaiah 54:6, translated in the New International Version like this:

> "The LORD will call you back
> as if you were a wife deserted and distressed in spirit—
> a wife who married young,
> only to be rejected," says your God.

God's provision for healing the wound of rejection is recorded in Matthew 27:46, 50, which describes the culmination of the agony of Jesus:

> About the ninth hour Jesus cried out with a loud voice, saying, "Eli, Eli, lama sabachthani?" that is, *"My God, My God, why have You forsaken Me?"*. . . Jesus, when He had cried out again with a loud voice, yielded up His spirit.

For the first time in the history of the universe, the Son of God called out to His Father and received no response. So fully was Jesus identified with man's iniquity that the uncompromising holiness of God caused Him to reject even His own Son. In this way Jesus endured rejection in its most agonizing form: rejection by a father. Almost immediately afterward He died—not of the wounds of crucifixion, but of a heart broken by rejection.

The record of Matthew continues immediately: "And behold, the veil of the temple was torn in two from top to bottom" (verse 51). Symbolically this demonstrated that the way had been opened for sinful man to enjoy direct fellowship with a holy God. The rejection of Jesus had opened the way for us to be accepted by God as His children. This is summed up by Paul in Ephesians 1:5–6: "Having predestined us to adoption as sons by Jesus Christ to Himself, . . . He [God] made us accepted in the Beloved." The rejection of Jesus resulted in our acceptance.

God's remedy for shame and rejection has never been more desperately needed than it is today. I estimate that at least one-quarter of the adults in the world today suffer from wounds of shame or rejection. It has given me measureless joy to point such people to the healing that flows from the cross of Jesus.

The two emotional aspects of the exchange at the cross that I have analyzed in this section may be summarized as follows:

Jesus bore our shame that we might share His glory.
Jesus endured our rejection that we might have His acceptance
  with the Father.

We Receive Blessing

The aspects of the exchange we have looked at so far cover some of humanity's most basic and urgent needs, but they are by no means exhaustive. Actually, there is no need resulting from man's rebellion that is not covered by the same principle of exchange: The evil came on Jesus that the good might be offered to us. Once we have learned to apply this principle in our lives, it releases God's provision for every need.

There remains for us to discuss one final, climactic aspect of the exchange, described by Paul in Galatians 3:13–14:

> Christ has redeemed us from the curse of the law, having become a curse for us (for it is written, "Cursed is everyone who hangs on a tree"), that the blessing of Abraham might come upon the Gentiles in Christ Jesus, that we might receive the promise of the Spirit through faith.

Paul applies to Jesus on the cross an enactment of the law of Moses, stated in Deuteronomy 21:23, according to which a person executed by hanging on a "tree" (a wooden gibbet) thereby came under the curse of God. Then he points to the resulting opposite: the blessing.

It does not require a theologian to analyze this aspect of the exchange:

Jesus became a curse
  that we might enter into the blessing.

The curse that came on Jesus is defined as "the curse of the law." In Deuteronomy 28, Moses gives an exhaustive list of both the blessings that result from obeying the law and the curses that result from breaking it. The curses listed in Deuteronomy 28:15–68 may be summed up as follows:

Humiliation
Barrenness, unfruitfulness
Mental and physical sickness
Family breakdown
Poverty
Defeat
Oppression
Failure
God's disfavor

Do some of these words apply to areas in your life? Are there things that rest like a dark shadow over you, shutting out the sunlight of God's blessing that you long for? If so, it may be that the root cause of your problems is a curse from which you need to be released.

To appreciate the full horror of the curse that came on Jesus, try to picture Him as He hung there on the cross.

Jesus had been rejected by His own countrymen, betrayed by one of His disciples and abandoned by the rest (though some returned later to observe His final agony). He was suspended naked between earth and heaven. His body was wracked by the pain of innumerable wounds, His soul weighed down by the guilt of all humanity. Earth had rejected Him and heaven would not respond to His cry. As the sun withdrew its light and darkness covered Him, His lifeblood ebbed out onto the dusty, stony soil. Yet out of the darkness, just before He expired, there came one final, triumphant cry: "It is finished!"

In the Greek text the phrase *It is finished!* consists of only one word. It is the perfect tense of a verb that means "to make something complete or perfect." In English it could be rendered "It is completely complete" or "It is perfectly perfect."

Jesus had taken on Himself every evil consequence that rebellion had brought on humanity. He had exhausted every curse of God's broken law. All this, that we in turn might receive every blessing due to His obedience. Such a sacrifice is stupendous in its scope, yet marvelous in its simplicity.

eight

Responding to God's Provision

HAVE YOU BEEN ABLE to accept with faith this account of the sacrifice of Jesus and all that He has obtained for you? Are you now eager to enter into God's full provision?

There is one barrier we must all deal with: the barrier of unforgiven sin. Do you already have a clear assurance that your sins have been forgiven because of the sacrifice of Jesus? If not, that is where you must begin. You can offer just a simple prayer:

> God, I acknowledge that I am a sinner and that there is unforgiven sin in my life. But I believe that Jesus was punished that I might be forgiven, and so I ask you now: Forgive all my sins, in Jesus' name.

God's Word promises that "if we confess our sins, He is faithful and just to forgive us our sins and to cleanse us from all unrighteousness" (1 John 1:9). Take God at His Word! This very moment believe that He has indeed forgiven you for all your sins.

There is one simple response you need to make—a response that is the simplest and purest expression of true faith. It is to say, "Thank You!"

Do that right now. Say, "Thank You, Lord Jesus, that You were punished that I might be forgiven. I do not fully understand, but I do believe and am grateful."

With the barrier of sin removed, the way is open for you to enter into all the other provisions God has made through the cross. Each one, just like the forgiveness of sin, must be received by simple faith in God's Word.

Every one of us has special needs and must come to God individually to accept His provision. Here is a general form of words you may use to claim any of the other provisions described in this chapter:

Lord Jesus, I thank You that You were wounded that I might be healed.

Lord Jesus, I thank You that You were made sin with my sinfulness that I might be made righteous with Your righteousness.

Lord Jesus, I thank You that You died my death that I might receive Your life.

Lord Jesus, I thank You that You endured my poverty that I might share Your abundance.

Lord Jesus, I thank You that You bore my shame that I might share Your glory.

Lord Jesus, I thank You that You suffered my rejection that I might have Your acceptance with the Father.

Lord Jesus, I thank You that You were made a curse that I might enter into the blessing.

Each provision you have prayed for is progressive. Your initial prayer has released God's power into your life. But that is merely the starting point. In order to appropriate the full provision you are seeking, you will need to do three things:

1. Search out these truths for yourself in the Bible.
2. Continually reaffirm the particular aspect of the exchange that answers your need.
3. Continually reaffirm your faith by thanking God for what He has provided.

The more you thank God, the more you will believe what He has done for you. And the more you believe, the more you will want to thank Him. These two actions—believing and thanking, thanking and believing—are like a spiral staircase that will take you continually higher into the fullness of God's provision.

The Exchange Made at the Cross

There is one—and only one—all-sufficient basis for every provision of God's mercy: the exchange that took place on the cross.

Jesus was *punished* that we might be *forgiven.*

Jesus was *wounded* that we might be *healed.*

Jesus was made *sin with our sinfulness* that we might be made *righteous with His righteousness.*

Jesus died our *death* that we might receive His *life.*

Jesus endured our *poverty* that we might share His *abundance.*

Jesus bore our *shame* that we might share His *glory.*

Jesus endured our *rejection* that we might have His *acceptance* with the Father.

Jesus was made a *curse* that we might enter into the *blessing*.

This list is not complete. There are other aspects of the exchange that could be added. But all of them are different facets of the provision God has made through the sacrifice of Jesus. The Bible sums them up in one grand, all-inclusive word: *salvation.* Christians often limit salvation to the experience of having one's sins forgiven and being born again. Wonderful though this is, it is only the first part of the total salvation revealed in the New Testament.

May I now offer you a prayer by which you can appropriate each of these exchanges for yourself?

Heavenly Father, I thank You for providing this wonderful divine exchange. I receive now by faith every portion of this perfect work.

I declare that since Jesus was punished for my sin, I now receive total forgiveness.

Christ was wounded, and I receive by faith the healing He has purchased for me.

I thank You, Father, that Christ was made sin for me, and I receive the gift of His perfect righteousness.

Since Christ died my death, I declare that I now share His life.

I believe that Christ bore the curse of poverty for me that I may share His abundance.

I believe that all my shame was borne on the cross, that I may share Christ's glory. I receive it by faith.

I place all my rejection on Christ, that I may receive the warm, total acceptance of my heavenly Father.

Thank You, Father, that Your Son was cursed that I may be blessed.

I believe You, Father, to make every aspect of the divine exchange real and practical in my life, for I "have received not the spirit of the world, but the Spirit who is from God, that [I] might know the things freely given to [me] by God" (1 Corinthians 2:12).

Thank You, Father. In Jesus' name. Amen.

PART 3

WHO IS THE HOLY SPIRIT?

ONE OF THE MOST important themes in my life has been the importance of the place of the Holy Spirit. Indeed, from the moment of my supernatural conversion in a British Army barrack room some sixty years ago, the Holy Spirit has been a real and precious Friend and Guide. I would never have come to the place in life I enjoy today without a vital relationship with the Holy Spirit *as a Person.* "All who are being led by the Spirit of God, these are sons of God" (Romans 8:14, NASB).

Join me in this important section as I unfold the main aspects of the identity, gifts and nature of the Holy Spirit.

nine

A PERSON—AND NOT A PERSON

THE BIBLE REPRESENTS the divinely inspired revelation of God. But God is so much "other" than we are that at times it becomes necessary to adjust or expand our usual forms of speech in order to communicate the Bible's revelation of God.

In Him both oneness and plurality are eternally combined. This mystery confronts us in the opening verse of the Bible (NKJV, here and throughout Part 3, except where noted): "In the beginning God created the heavens and the earth." In the original Hebrew, *elohim* (the word for "God") is plural in form, but the verb *bara* ("created") is singular. In other words, both oneness and plurality are combined.

Further on, in Genesis 1:26, we are again confronted with the combination of singular and plural in reference to God: "Then God said, 'Let Us make man in Our image, according

59

to Our likeness. . . .'" The verb *said* is singular in form, but the pronouns *Us* and *Our* are plural.

This combination of singular and plural in reference to God recurs in other passages of Scripture. The prophet Isaiah had a vision of the Lord on His throne and then heard Him say, "Whom shall I send, and who will go for Us?" (Isaiah 6:8). The pronoun *I* implies that one Person is speaking, but the pronoun *Us* indicates that He is speaking on behalf of more than one Person.

In the ongoing revelation of Scripture, three distinct Persons emerge, each of whom is God—God the Father, God the Son and God the Holy Spirit. The first of the three divine Persons referred to individually in Scripture is the Spirit: "The Spirit of God was moving over the surface of the waters" (Genesis 1:2, NASB).

We can never explain God, but He has provided us in the world He has created with various parables that reveal Himself. One of these is light. Light is part of everyday life to which we do not normally give much thought. Yet in this single phenomenon we discern plurality in at least two forms.

Light is regularly refracted into the three primary colors: blue, yellow and red. Again, in the rainbow, light appears in seven colors: violet, indigo, blue, green, yellow, orange, red. Thus, within the unity of light, there is the trinity of the primary colors and the sevenfold diversity of the rainbow.

Throughout Scripture seven is the number particularly associated with the Holy Spirit. Revelation 4:5 speaks of "the seven Spirits of God." In Isaiah 11:1–2 the prophet shows how the Holy Spirit will set apart Jesus as the Messiah (the Anointed One) and lists seven distinct aspects of the Holy Spirit: the Spirit of the Lord (the Spirit who speaks in the first person as God); the Spirit of wisdom; the Spirit of understanding; the Spirit of counsel; the Spirit of strength; the Spirit of knowledge; and the Spirit of the fear of the Lord.

It is significant that, even in Jesus Himself, knowledge needs to be balanced by the fear of the Lord. Otherwise knowledge on its own can become a source of pride. "Knowledge puffs up [makes arrogant]" (1 Corinthians 8:1).

In Acts 13:2 the Holy Spirit is plainly presented as being Himself God. To the leaders of the church in Antioch, "The Holy Spirit said, 'Now separate to Me Barnabas and Saul for the work to which I have called them.'" Clearly the Spirit is speaking here in the first person as God.

God's Total Involvement in Man's Redemption

Perhaps the supreme revelation of God's grace is His plan to provide redemption for the fallen human race through the sacrifice of Jesus. As I studied the details of this divine plan, I made an exciting discovery: In every stage of redemption each Person of the Godhead played a unique and distinctive part, as indicated by the following outline:

1. **The conception of Jesus.** God the Father caused Jesus to be conceived in the womb of Mary by the Holy Spirit (see Luke 1:35).
2. **The beginning of the ministry of Jesus.** When Jesus submitted Himself to the baptism of John, the Holy Spirit descended on Him in the form of a dove and the Father acknowledged Him as His Son (see Luke 3:21–22).
3. **The ongoing ministry of Jesus.** Peter sums this up in Acts 10:38: "God [the Father] anointed Jesus of Nazareth with the Holy Spirit and with power, who went about doing good and healing all who were oppressed by the devil. . . ."
4. **The sacrifice of Jesus on the cross.** "Christ . . . through the eternal [Holy] Spirit offered Himself without spot to God [the Father] . . ." (see Hebrews 9:14).
5. **The resurrection of Jesus.** God the Father resurrected Jesus by the power of the Holy Spirit (see Romans 1:4; 8:11).

6. **Pentecost.** Exalted to the right hand of God the Father, Jesus received from Him the gift of the Holy Spirit and poured it out on the waiting disciples (see Acts 2:33).

In each stage of redemption, the Holy Spirit played His own vital and distinctive role. He is rightly called both "the Spirit of grace" and "the Spirit of glory"—grace, that is, that leads to glory (see Hebrews 10:29; 1 Peter 4:14).

Both Personal and Non-Personal

Another unique fact about the Holy Spirit stretches our powers of comprehension. The Spirit is both personal and non-personal—both a "He" and an "it."

The language in which the New Testament has come to us is Greek, which has three genders: masculine (he), feminine (she), neuter (it). Grammatically the Greek word for "spirit," *pneuma,* is neuter. The appropriate pronoun would, therefore, be neuter—i.e., *it.* Both *He* and *it,* however, are applied to the Holy Spirit (but never *she*). In John 16:13, for example, the rules of Greek grammar are deliberately set aside to emphasize that the Holy Spirit is a "He" as well as an "it": "When He, the Spirit of truth, has come. . . ."

Like English, Greek uses the definite article, corresponding to our English *the.* (Some other languages—for example, Latin and Russian—have no corresponding word.) In the Greek New Testament, the phrase *Holy Spirit* is sometimes preceded by the definite article (corresponding to *the)* and sometimes not. In English this would amount to the difference between *the Holy Spirit* and *Holy Spirit.*

To English ears, however, the phrase *Holy Spirit* on its own sounds incomplete. All English translations invariably insert *the* before *Holy Spirit,* therefore, even when it does not appear in the original Greek. Only by consulting the Greek text is it possible to determine whether *the* is actually there.

Through my study of the Greek New Testament, I have come to the conclusion that the presence or absence of *the* in conjunction with the Holy Spirit marks an important distinction. When *Holy Spirit* is not preceded by *the,* it denotes something nonpersonal—life, or a power, a force, a presence, an influence. When *Holy Spirit* is preceded by *the,* on the other hand, He is being depicted as a Person.

Consider one distinctive mark of personality: the ability to speak. At Pentecost, when the Holy Spirit descended from heaven, He spoke in other tongues through the disciples. By this He signified that He had come, as a Person, to take up His dwelling on earth. He is the permanent, personal representative of the Godhead residing on earth.

Ever since Pentecost, each time the Holy Spirit comes to take up His residence as a Person in the body of a believer, it is appropriate that He should manifest His presence by speaking out of that believer in a new language imparted supernaturally. In effect He is saying, "Now you know that I am here as a Person to indwell your body."

For this reason, in 1 Corinthians 6:19 Paul prefixes onto *Holy Spirit* the definite article: "Do you not know that your body is the temple of *the* Holy Spirit?" (emphasis added). Paul is stressing that speaking in tongues is not merely a brief supernatural experience, but a divinely given sign that the Holy Spirit, as a Person, has taken up His dwelling in the believer's body, thereby making it a sacred temple. This places a solemn obligation on each believer to keep his or her body in a condition of holiness that is appropriate for God's temple.

The definite article is also prefixed when the Holy Spirit is depicted as exercising authority in the Church—for example, sending out apostles, appointing elders or directing apostolic ministries. But when people are being baptized in, or filled with, the Holy Spirit, the definite article is usually omitted. This indicates to me that the Holy Spirit is seen in those places as something non-personal—as life, or power, or an influence.

The first of the following two lists consists of passages in which *the* is prefixed to *Holy Spirit;* the second, in which *Holy Spirit* occurs without *the*.

With "the" Prefixed

The following are some of the passages where *the* is prefixed to *Holy Spirit:*

Matthew 12:32: "Whoever speaks against the Holy Spirit, it will not be forgiven him" (see Mark 3:29).

Mark 13:11: "It is not you who speak, but the Holy Spirit."

Luke 3:22: "The Holy Spirit descended in bodily form like a dove upon Him. . . ."

Luke 12:12: "The Holy Spirit will teach you . . . what you ought to say."

John 14:26: "The Helper, the Holy Spirit, . . . He will teach you all things. . . ."

Acts 2:38: "You shall receive the gift of the Holy Spirit."

Acts 5:3: "Ananias, why has Satan filled your heart to lie to the Holy Spirit? . . ."

Acts 13:2: "The Holy Spirit said, 'Now separate to Me Barnabas and Saul for the work to which I have called them.'"

Acts 13:4: "So, being sent out by the Holy Spirit, they went. . . ."

Acts 15:28: "It seemed good to the Holy Spirit, and to us."

Acts 16:6: "They were forbidden by the Holy Spirit to preach the word in Asia."

Acts 20:28: "Take heed . . . to all the flock, among which the Holy Spirit has made you overseers. . . ."

Acts 21:11: "Thus says the Holy Spirit. . . ."

1 Corinthians 6:19: "Do you not know that your body is the temple of the Holy Spirit who is in you . . . ?"

Without "the" Prefixed

Here are some passages where *the* is omitted. Although these are quoted from the New King James Version, I have omitted the *the* to underscore how they actually read in the Greek.

Matthew 1:18: "She was found with child of Holy Spirit."

Matthew 3:11: "He will baptize you with Holy Spirit and fire" (see Mark 1:8; Luke 3:16; John 1:33; Acts 1:5).

Luke 1:15: "He [John the Baptist] will also be filled with Holy Spirit, even from his mother's womb" (see Luke 1:41, 67; 4:1; Acts 2:4; 6:3, 5; 9:17; 13:9, 52).

Luke 1:35: "Holy Spirit will come upon you [Mary]."

John 20:22: "He breathed on them, and said to them, 'Receive Holy Spirit [or holy breath].'"

Acts 10:38: "God anointed Jesus of Nazareth with Holy Spirit and with power. . . ."

Romans 14:17: "The kingdom of God is . . . righteousness and peace and joy in Holy Spirit."

Romans 15:13: ". . . That you may abound in hope by the power of Holy Spirit."

Romans 15:16: "The offering of the Gentiles . . . sanctified by Holy Spirit."

1 Corinthians 12:3: "No one can say that Jesus is Lord except by Holy Spirit."

Titus 3:5: ". . . Washing of regeneration and renewing of Holy Spirit . . ."

Hebrews 2:4: ". . . Various miracles, and gifts [literally, distributions] of Holy Spirit . . ."

Hebrews 6:4: ". . . And have become partakers of Holy Spirit . . ."

2 Peter 1:21: "Holy men . . . spoke as they were moved [borne along] by Holy Spirit."

Jude 20: ". . . Praying in Holy Spirit . . ."

Finally, here are just a few of the many titles given in Scripture to the Holy Spirit: *the Spirit of grace; the Spirit of glory; the Spirit of wisdom; the Spirit of truth; the Spirit of self-discipline.*

Meditate on the significance of each and search out some others for yourself. Then take time to thank Jesus that He has fulfilled His promise to send us the Holy Spirit.

ten

ETERNAL, OMNISCIENT, OMNIPRESENT

IN THIS CHAPTER we will look at three profoundly significant adjectives that apply to the Holy Spirit: *eternal, omniscient, omnipresent.*

Eternal

At the close of one of the first Pentecostal services I ever attended, the preacher asked me, "Do you believe you're a sinner?"

At that time I was a professional philosopher and had just completed my dissertation on "definitions" at Cambridge University. I immediately ran over in my mind various possible definitions of a sinner. All of them applied to me exactly. So I answered, "Yes, I do believe I'm a sinner."

"Do you believe Christ died for your sins?"

I thought this over. "To tell you the truth, I can't see what the death of Jesus Christ nineteen centuries ago could have to do with the sins that I've committed in my lifetime."

The preacher was wise enough not to argue with me, but I am sure he prayed for me!

A few days later I had a powerful encounter with Jesus Christ, which changed the course of my life. In particular the Bible became a living, meaningful book.

Some time later I was reading in Hebrews 9:14 that "Christ . . . through *the eternal Spirit* offered Himself without spot to God" (emphasis added). Suddenly I grasped the significance of the word *eternal*. Its meaning is far broader than just something lasting an extremely long time. It denotes something that is above and beyond the limitations of time—something that simultaneously comprehends the past, the present and the future.

When Jesus offered Himself on the cross, His sacrifice was not limited to the time at which He died. It encompassed the sins of all human beings of all ages—past, present and future. It included the sins I was to commit nineteen centuries later!

The Greek adjective *eternal* has a fathomless depth of meaning. It is derived from the noun *aion,* from which we get the English word *aeon.* An *aion* is a measurement of time and occurs in a variety of expressions, as in the following literal translations:

Galatians 1:5: "Unto the ages of the ages" ("forever and ever")

Hebrews 7:24: "For the age" ("forever")—that is, for the duration of the present age

Jude 25: "From before every age, and now, and unto all the ages" ("both now and forever")

It becomes obvious that English translations do not begin to convey the depth of the meaning of the Greek phrases. The expressions above, and others like them, fill me with a sense of awe. I feel like a drop of moisture suspended above a bottomless chasm that separates two mountains too high for me to climb. My mind cannot fully comprehend that there could be even one age made up of ages, much less that there are ages made up of such ages. Yet the eternal Holy Spirit encompasses them all, stretching from the measureless past on into the measureless future.

I begin to apprehend in a new way the title under which God is endlessly worshiped in heaven: "Lord God Almighty, who [eternally] was and is and is to come!" (Revelation 4:8).

Omniscient

Closely related to the *eternal* nature of the Holy Spirit is His *omniscience.* In 1 John 3:20 the apostle confronts us with a profound yet simple revelation: *God knows all things.* From the tiniest insect on the earth to the farthest star in the galaxy, there is nothing God does not know completely. He also knows things about us that we do not know about ourselves—for instance, the number of hairs that each of us has on our heads (see Matthew 10:30).

God knew the number of inhabitants in the city of Nineveh (see Jonah 4:11). He knew—and controlled—the growth of the plant that shaded Jonah. He also knew—and controlled—the action of the worm that caused the plant to wither (see Jonah 4:6–7).

In 1 Corinthians 2:9–10 Paul speaks about the things God has prepared that "eye has not seen, nor ear heard, nor have entered into the heart of man." Then he continues, "But God has revealed them to us through His Spirit. *For the Spirit searches all things,* yes, the deep things of God" (emphasis added). The Holy Spirit plumbs the deepest depths and scales the highest heights of all that was, that is and that is to come. His knowledge is infinite.

It is in the light of this infinite knowledge that we must each be prepared to account for ourselves to God. "There is no creature hidden from His sight, but all things are naked and open to the eyes of Him to whom we must give account" (Hebrews 4:13).

The supernatural knowledge and wisdom of the Holy Spirit were manifested throughout the earthly ministry of Jesus, but never more than in His dealings with Judas Iscariot. When the disciples told Jesus, "We have come to believe and know that You are the Christ [Messiah], the Son of the living God" (John 6:69), the Lord gave them an answer revealing that being the Messiah would entail being betrayed by one of His own followers: "'Did I not choose you, the twelve, and one of you is a devil?' He spoke of Judas Iscariot, the son of Simon, for it was he who would betray Him, being one of the twelve" (John 6:70–71). Jesus knew by the Holy Spirit long before Judas did that he would eventually betray Him, even before that disciple knew it himself!

Even so, Judas could not carry out his plan until Jesus spoke a word that released him to do so. At the Last Supper Jesus warned His disciples, "One of you will betray Me." When questioned who it would be, Jesus replied,

> "It is he to whom I shall give a piece of bread when I have dipped it." And having dipped the bread, He gave it to Judas Iscariot, the son of Simon.
>
> Now after the piece of bread, Satan entered him. Then Jesus said to him, "What you do, do quickly."
>
> John 13:26–27

Having received the piece of bread, Judas went out quickly to betray Jesus (verse 30). Jesus Himself spoke the word that released him to do it. Throughout this whole scene, it was the Betrayed, not the betrayer, who was in control.

When we comprehend the completeness of God's knowledge—and in particular His foreknowledge—it assures us that no matter what happens, God is never taken by surprise. There is no such thing as an emergency in the kingdom of heaven. Not only does God know the end from the beginning, but He Himself *is* both "the Beginning and the End" (Revelation 21:6). And He is always in total control.

In particular, God knows those He has chosen to be with Him in eternity: "Whom He foreknew, He also predestined to be conformed to the image of His Son, that He might be the firstborn among many brethren" (Romans 8:29).

If by the mercy and grace of God we make it through to that glorious, eternal destination, Jesus will never greet anyone with the words, "I never expected to see *you* here!" Rather, He will say, "My child, I've been waiting for you. We couldn't sit down to the marriage feast until you came." At that glorious banquet every place setting, I believe, will carry the name of the person for whom it is prepared.

Until the number of the redeemed is complete, God waits with amazing patience, "not willing that any should perish but that all should come to repentance" (2 Peter 3:9).

Omnipresent

next Lesson

When we say that God is *omnipresent,* we mean that He is present everywhere at the same time. In Jeremiah 23:23–24 God Himself affirms this:

> "Am I a God near at hand," says the LORD,
> "And not a God afar off?
> Can anyone hide himself in secret places,
> So I shall not see him?" says the LORD;
> "Do I not fill heaven and earth?" says the LORD.

How can this be? We know that God is seated on His throne in heaven, with Jesus at His right hand. How then can He fill heaven and earth with His presence?

In Psalm 139 David supplies the answer. First he asks, "Where can I go from Your Spirit? Or where can I flee from Your presence?" (verse 7), revealing that it is through His Spirit that God makes Himself present everywhere at the same time. Then David fills in the vivid details:

> If I ascend into heaven, You are there;
> If I make my bed in hell, behold, You are there.
> If I take the wings of the morning,
> And dwell in the uttermost parts of the sea,
> Even there Your hand shall lead me,
> And Your right hand shall hold me.
> If I say, "Surely the darkness shall fall on me,"
> Even the night shall be light about me;
> Indeed, the darkness shall not hide from You,
> But the night shines as the day;
> The darkness and the light are both alike to You.
>
> verses 8–12

No matter where we go, God is present by His Spirit—invisible, often imperceptible but inescapable. For the unbeliever this may be a terrifying thought, but for the believer it is a comforting, strengthening assurance. No matter where we may find ourselves, "even there Your hand shall lead me, and Your right hand shall hold me."

In the New Testament Jesus Himself gives us this assurance: "I will never leave you nor forsake you" (Hebrews 13:5). At times we may be in no way conscious of His presence, but by His Holy Spirit He is there. Our surroundings may appear totally dark, but "the darkness shall not hide from You . . ."

Each of us needs to cultivate an inner sensitivity to the Holy Spirit that does not depend on the evidence of our physical senses. When our senses tell us nothing about His presence, or even when they seem to deny it, there should be an area in the inmost depths of our spirit that maintains an uninterrupted awareness of the Holy Spirit's presence. Then we shall understand more fully why He is given the title of "the Comforter" or "the Helper" (John 14:26, KJV and NKJV).

In the next chapter I will speak about the ministry of the Holy Spirit in the Church. But there is no more appropriate way to close this chapter than by thanking the Father and the Son for sending us the Holy Spirit. Will you join with me?

eleven

∞

SELF-EFFACING SERVANT, CONSUMING FIRE

THE HOLY SPIRIT has chosen to reveal Himself through the Scriptures. What do they tell us about Him?

The primary revelation of the Holy Spirit is contained in His title: He is *Holy.* This is the standard by which we must judge every message, every manifestation, every movement that claims to be of God's Spirit: *Is it compatible with His holiness?*

From "Pentecostal" to "Charismatic"

Someone has said that familiarity breeds contempt. Unfortunately, this sometimes applies to the things of the Spirit—in particular, to the development of the Pentecostal movement. When the baptism and gifts of the Spirit first made an impact on the Church in the early years of the twentieth century, it was neither fashionable nor popular to be labeled *Pentecostal.* There was a stigma attached to it, a price to be paid.

The early Pentecostals were not, for the most part, highly educated. They came from "the wrong side of the tracks." Some of the things they said and did were foolish. Their concept of holiness was often legalistic. But they paid a price. Their experience did not come cheaply.

In the course of the twentieth century this changed, particularly with the advent of the charismatic renewal. The substitution of the label *charismatic* for *Pentecostal* somehow seemed to make it more respectable. It became fashionable in some circles to be charismatic.

To these developments there was both a plus and a minus. On the plus side, the baptism and gifts of the Holy Spirit have been made accessible to the whole Body of Christ. But on the minus side, there are ministries and practices to which the word *holy* can no longer be applied. Here are just a few examples:

1. Flippant and irreverent language applied to the sacred things of God
2. Public ministries motivated by barefaced covetousness and bolstered by claims that are not substantiated or promises that are not fulfilled
3. Bizarre and unseemly manifestations attributed to the Holy Spirit

That these elements are found in ministries that claim to be Christian does not surprise me. After all, covetousness and self-serving are deeply rooted in human nature. What does astonish me is that millions of professing Christians apparently accept that kind of behavior as proceeding from the Holy Spirit!

Who Is the Holy Spirit?

Obviously the time has come for us to take a fresh look at the Holy Spirit. What kind of Person is He?

75

A Humble, Self-Effacing Servant

I can still recall what a shock it was for me when I first realized that servanthood is part of the divine nature. Most people today regard being a servant as a task to be avoided, something menial and degrading. This attitude is one of the corrupting influences poisoning our contemporary culture.

Servanthood originated not in time but in eternity, not on earth but in heaven. Eternally Jesus the Son is the joyful, willing, obedient Servant of God the Father. The Holy Spirit, in turn, is the obedient, self-effacing Servant of the Father and the Son. He does not complain of victimization or demand His rights. He fulfills His appointed role perfectly. He is the Servant God!

This is beautifully illustrated in Genesis 24, which describes how Abraham went about obtaining a bride for his son Isaac. There are four beautiful "types" in this account. Abraham is a type of God the Father; Isaac is a type of God's Son, Jesus; Rebekah is a type of the bride of Christ, the Church. And what about Abraham's servant? Although never given a name, he is the main character. Abraham's servant is a type of the Holy Spirit. As a servant, he had one supreme objective: to find the young woman who was to become the bride of his master, to equip and adorn her, and to escort her safely to the bridegroom.

It was for a similar purpose that the Holy Spirit came to earth at Pentecost. He is here with one supreme objective: to find, equip and adorn the bride of Christ, the Church, to escort her safely through this world and to present her to Jesus—a pure and spotless bride.

One main characteristic of the Holy Spirit is that He never attracts attention to Himself. Here are literal translations of some of what Jesus told us about Him: "He will testify of Me" (John 15:26); "He will not speak on His own authority, but whatever He hears He will speak" (John 16:13); "He will take of what is Mine and declare it to you" (John 16:14).

More remarkable still, in all the revelation that the Holy Spirit has given us in Scripture, *there is no record that anyone ever addressed a prayer to the Holy Spirit.* The pattern prayer that Jesus gave His disciples is addressed to the Father. To this prayer Jesus added His own promise: "Whatever you ask in My name, that I will do, that the Father may be glorified in the Son" (John 14:13).

The terminus of all scriptural prayer is God the Father. The ministry of the Holy Spirit is to help us reach the Father with our prayers, not to offer us an alternative destination. We are to pray *in* the Spirit (see Ephesians 6:18), not *to* the Spirit.

In recent years, however, some sections of the Church have deviated from this scriptural pattern. The focus has shifted from the Father and the Son to the Spirit. Many songs—with little scriptural content—are directed to the Holy Spirit. Often the main emphasis has been on subjective experiences that cater to the egos of those participating. This subtle, unadvertised shift of emphasis has opened God's people to spiritual dangers that many fail to discern.

We need to keep in mind two basic principles. First, the Holy Spirit never caters to the human ego. Second, the Holy Spirit never attracts attention to Himself. He always directs our focus to Jesus. Whenever these principles are set aside, the result may be fleshly excitement and emotional self-indulgence without any genuine holiness. Or, more dangerous still, it may open the way for a satanic counterfeit that in turn opens the way for the activity of demons.

A Consuming Fire

One way the Holy Spirit manifests Himself at times is *fire.* In fact, the last time the Holy Spirit appears visibly in Scripture is as "seven lamps of fire . . . burning before the throne" of God (Revelation 4:5).

The writer of Hebrews makes a simple but profound statement: "Our God is a consuming fire" (12:29). He does not say God is *like* a fire, but that God *is* a fire. For this reason "we may serve God acceptably with reverence and godly fear"

(Hebrews 12:28)—not slavish fear, but "the fear of the LORD [which] is clean, enduring forever" (Psalm 19:9). The writer of Hebrews is not speaking of God the Father or of God the Son, but of God the Holy Spirit. He actually is a fire—a consuming fire.

At various points in the history of Israel, the Holy Spirit came down among the people as a fire. In the Tabernacle in the wilderness, when Aaron had offered all the appointed sacrifices, "fire came out from before the LORD and consumed the burnt offering and the fat on the altar. When all the people saw it, they shouted and fell on their faces" (Leviticus 9:24).

Again, when Solomon had finished praying at the dedication of his temple, "fire came down from heaven and consumed the burnt offering and the sacrifices; and the glory of the LORD filled the temple. And the priests could not enter the house of the LORD, because the glory of the LORD had filled the LORD's house" (2 Chronicles 7:1–2).

Later, in a time of apostasy, when the Lord responded to Elijah's prayer on Mount Carmel, "the fire of the LORD fell and consumed the burnt sacrifice, and the wood and the stones and the dust, and it licked up the water that was in the trench. Now when all the people saw it, they fell on their faces; and they said, 'The LORD, He is God! The LORD, He is God!'" (1 Kings 18:38–39).

Each time the fire came down and the people fell on their faces, they were not simply moved by a spiritual manifestation. They were responding to the presence of God—God the Holy Spirit—who had come down among them as a consuming fire. In His presence they were physically incapable of standing.

To Purify or to Destroy?

There are two opposite sides to fire. Fire can be beneficial but also dangerous. Fire can purify but also destroy. So it is with the fire of the Holy Spirit. He can minister God's blessing and favor on those who are obedient. But He can also minister God's wrath and judgment on those who are presumptuous and self-willed.

Immediately after the account of the fire that fell on Aaron's sacrifice in the Tabernacle, the record continues:

> Nadab and Abihu, the sons of Aaron, each took his censer and put fire in it, put incense on it, and offered profane fire before the LORD, which He had not commanded them. So fire went out from the LORD and devoured them, and they died before the LORD.
>
> Leviticus 10:1–2

What a solemn lesson! The same fire that brought God's blessing on Aaron's sacrifice, offered in obedience, brought instant death to his two sons when they went into God's presence with "profane" or unholy fire.

God has already defined the way in which we are to approach Him: "with reverence and godly fear" (Hebrews 12:28). Both Jews and Gentiles "have access *by one Spirit* to the Father" (Ephesians 2:18, emphasis added).

To offer "profane fire" is to approach God with presumption and self-will in any spirit that is not the Holy Spirit. It is, therefore, a matter of vital importance—in fact, of life and death—to recognize the Holy Spirit in whatever way He manifests Himself and to distinguish Him from any other counterfeit spirit.

Of all the Israelites, Nadab and Abihu, Aaron's sons, might have felt they had a special privilege to enter God's presence by a way of their own choosing. By right of birth, Nadab should have succeeded Aaron as high priest. But there is no substitute for obeying God's Word—neither denominational status nor dramatic miracles nor crowd appeal. God does not have a special privileged elite who can ignore His requirements without suffering the consequences.

God's judgment on the self-exaltation of Nadab and Abihu shows us that the Holy Spirit imparts His blessing only to those who meet His requirements. His requirements today are, first, to focus on exalting and glorifying the Lord Jesus Christ; and second, to carefully follow the directions that the Spirit Himself has transmitted to us in the Scriptures.

twelve

THE SPIRIT OF TRUTH

"I will pray the Father, and He will give you another Helper, that He may abide with you forever—the Spirit of truth, whom the world cannot receive, because it neither sees Him nor knows Him; but you know Him, for He dwells with you and will be in you."

John 14:16–17

WHEN JESUS PROMISED His disciples that He would ask the Father to send them a divine Helper, He gave this Helper a special name: "the Spirit of truth." At the same time, however, He warned them that the world would not be able to receive this Helper. Why not? The Scripture supplies two reasons.

First, from the time men and women turned away from God in rebellion, they have been unwilling to accept the truth that exposes their unrighteous deeds. Therefore they "suppress the truth in unrighteousness" (Romans 1:18). Second, rebellion against God has exposed humanity to the domination of the god of this age, "Satan, who deceives the whole world" (Revelation 12:9). Deception is the primary weapon Satan relies on to keep humanity under his control. Once his ability to deceive is stripped away, Satan has nothing to offer anyone except a place with him in the lake of eternal fire!

Over many centuries human philosophy has never been able to produce a satisfactory definition of "truth." The Bible, on the other hand, gives a threefold answer. First, Jesus said, "*I* am the truth" (John 14:6, emphasis added). Second, in praying to God the Father, Jesus said, "*Your word* is truth" (John 17:17, emphasis added). Third, John tells us, "*The [Holy] Spirit* is truth" (1 John 5:6, emphasis added).

In the spiritual realm, therefore, there are three coordinates of truth: *Jesus, the Scripture* and *the Holy Spirit.* When these three are in agreement, we know we have arrived at truth— absolute truth. It is important, however, that we check all three coordinates before we arrive at a conclusion. There are three questions we must ask concerning any spiritual issue:

Does it represent Jesus as He truly is?

Is it in harmony with Scripture?

Does the Holy Spirit bear His witness?

Historically the Church would have been spared many errors and deceptions if she had always checked all three coordinates of truth. It is not enough that a teacher paints an appealing picture of Jesus as a perfect moral example. Or that a pastor batters his congregation with a barrage of Scripture verses. Or that an evangelist impresses his audience with a thrilling display of supernatural gifts. Before we can accept what is presented to us as truth, all three coordinates must be in place: Jesus, the Scripture, the Holy Spirit.

In the threefold presentation of truth, the distinctive function of the Holy Spirit is to *bear witness:* "It is the Spirit who bears witness" (1 John 5:6). The Holy Spirit bears witness to Jesus as the eternal Son of God, who shed His blood on the cross as the all-sufficient sacrifice for our sins. In the words of Charles Wesley's great hymn "Arise, My Soul, Arise":

> The Spirit answers to the blood
> And tells me I am born of God.

The Holy Spirit also bears witness to the truth and authority of Scripture, as Paul wrote to the Thessalonians: "Our gospel did not come to you in word only, but also in power, and in the Holy Spirit and in much assurance . . ." (1 Thessalonians 1:5).

What Is Hypocrisy?

There can be no compromise between the Holy Spirit, who is the Spirit of Truth, and Satan, who "is a liar and the father of it" (John 8:44). This was dramatically demonstrated in the early Church, when Ananias and Sapphira lied about the money they had offered the Church. They claimed they had brought the full price of the property they had sold, whereas in fact they had kept back part of it.

The Spirit of truth in Peter was not deceived. He charged Ananias with lying not only to men but to the Holy Spirit Himself—the one who is the very Spirit of Truth:

> "Ananias, why has Satan filled your heart to lie to the Holy Spirit and keep back part of the price of the land for yourself? While it remained, was it not your own? And after it was sold, was it not in your own control? Why have you conceived this thing in your heart? You have not lied to men but to God." Then Ananias, hearing these words, fell down and breathed his last. So great fear came upon all those who heard these things.
>
> Acts 5:3–5

Three hours later Sapphira came in and repeated the same lie. Like her husband, she paid for it with her life.

Rightly defined, the sin of which Ananias and Sapphira were guilty was *hypocrisy*—religious pretense. They were pretending to be more generous and more committed to the Lord than they really were. Jesus reserved His strongest words of condemnation for this sin in the religious leaders of His day. Seven times in Matthew 23 He said to them, "Woe to you . . . hypocrites!"

Our English words *hypocrite* and *hypocrisy* are derived from the Greek word *hupokrites,* which means "actor." This is the essence of hypocrisy: putting on a religious act. Probably no sin is more common among religious people than hypocrisy. In fact, some forms of religion almost demand it.

When people enter a religious building, their whole demeanor changes. They are no longer natural, free and open. They appear to be gripped by some kind of invisible cramp and required to put on a religious mask. Different branches of religion may require different masks, but few of them allow people to be their real selves.

When the preacher condemns certain sins, such people respond with a dutiful "Amen!" But outside the church they commit those very sins without even a twinge of conscience. If they pray out loud, they use a special tone of voice and often a special vocabulary. They do not stop to consider how a human father would feel if his child were to address him with such artificial language or to put on an unnatural form of behavior just to impress him.

The God of the Bible has no time for hypocrites. This comes out very clearly in the story of Job. Job's three friends poured forth a torrent of religious platitudes. They said, in effect, "God always blesses the righteous; they never suffer unjustly." On the other hand, "God always judges the wicked; they never prosper." Yet the facts of history demonstrate that this is not true. It is just religious talk.

Job, on the other hand, was completely frank. He said, in effect, "God is not treating me fairly. I have done nothing to deserve all this. But even if He kills me, I will still trust Him."

In Job 42:7 the Lord revealed His estimate of the conduct of Job and his friends. He said to Eliphaz, "My wrath is aroused against you and your two friends, for you have not spoken of Me what is right, as My servant Job has" (Job 42:7).

We need to ask ourselves: How does this kind of religious behavior differ from the sin of Ananias and Sapphira, which cost them their lives?

The Moment of Truth

At a certain point in his career, King David was guilty of two terrible sins. First, he committed adultery with Bathsheba, the wife of his neighbor Uriah. Then, to cover up his sin, he procured the murder of Uriah.

Apparently David got away with all this. He still went through his regular forms of worship. He continued to carry out his duties as king. He still lived in the royal palace. Outwardly nothing had changed—until God's messenger, the prophet Nathan, confronted David with his sin. At that moment David's eternal destiny hung in the balance. By the grace of God, David made the right response. He offered no excuses, made no attempt to cover up. He acknowledged, "I have sinned" (2 Samuel 12:13).

Later, as he wrote in Psalm 51, David offered up a prayer of confession and then a cry for mercy. Verses 5 and 6 each begin with the word *Behold,* expressing a sudden revelation of a vital truth.

Verse 5: "Behold, I was brought forth in iniquity, and in sin my mother conceived me." David had come face to face with something that only the Spirit of Truth can reveal: not just the sinful acts he had committed, but the awful evil power of inherited sinfulness that indwells every descendant of Adam.

Verse 6 reveals the only basis on which God offers deliverance from the power of indwelling sin: "Behold, You desire *truth in the inward parts*" (emphasis added). Even after his sin,

David had continued to go through all the outward forms of behavior appropriate to his role as king. But now there was a vast gap between his outward behavior and the inward condition of his heart. He had become a hypocrite—an actor playing a part that no longer corresponded to what was in his heart. For this there was only one remedy: honest confession and wholehearted repentance.

From Palm Sunday to Good Friday

There is one truth that runs through the whole Bible: *God will never compromise with sin.* This is vividly illustrated by two days in the life of Jesus: Palm Sunday and Good Friday.

On Palm Sunday Jesus entered Jerusalem as a popular hero— "the prophet from Nazareth of Galilee" (Matthew 21:11). The whole city was open to Him. He could easily have set aside His bitter enemies, the religious leaders, and established Himself as King. That was what the people were longing for.

Yet He chose another way. Five days later He hung rejected and naked on a cruel cross. Why? Because God will never compromise with sin, and the only way to deal with sin was the sacrifice of Jesus on the cross.

Many Christians today are speaking and praying about "revival." They often overlook the fact that there is one barrier to revival that can never be bypassed. It is *sin.* Until sin is dealt with, true revival can never come. And there is only one way to deal with sin: "He who covers his sins will not prosper, but whoever confesses and forsakes them will have mercy" (Proverbs 28:13).

Many sections of the contemporary Church, frankly, are full of "covered sin." Here are some sins that Christians often seek to cover:

1. Abuse of a child—physical, emotional, sexual, or a combination.

2. Broken marriage vows.
3. Unethical dealings with money.
4. Addiction to pornography. (I have been shocked to discover how common this is among leaders in the Church.)
5. Gluttony—overindulgence of our physical appetites.

God's remedy is twofold: first *confess,* then *forsake.* It is seldom easy to confess our sins. Yet there is no other remedy. "If we confess our sins, He is faithful and just to forgive us our sins and to cleanse us from all unrighteousness" (1 John 1:9). God has never committed Himself to forgive sins that we are not willing to confess.

But it is not enough merely to confess. We must also "forsake." We must make a resolute determination not to continue to commit the sin we have confessed. We must follow the succinct advice that Daniel gave King Nebuchadnezzar: "Break off your sins by being righteous" (Daniel 4:27). Between righteousness and sin there is no middle ground. "All unrighteousness is sin" (1 John 5:17). Whatever is not righteous is sinful.

Are you face to face with a difficult decision? If this chapter has caused you to question some things in your life that you have been accepting, or it has confronted you with some area of disobedience, open up to the Spirit of truth. He is ready and willing to come to your help.

thirteen

∞

THE GIFTS OF THE SPIRIT

WHEN ABRAHAM SENT his servant from Canaan to Padan Aram to seek a bride for his son Isaac, the servant loaded ten camels to take with him. In the Middle East I have witnessed with my own eyes how much can be loaded onto a camel. It is amazing!

The ten loaded camels were visible evidence that Abraham was an honored, prosperous man. Included in their loads were precious gifts of jewelry. When the servant found the young woman who was to become Isaac's bride, his first act was to adorn her face with a very conspicuous nose jewel.

By accepting the gift, Rebekah committed herself to become Isaac's bride. Had she refused the gift, she would have rejected and dishonored Isaac. She could never have become his bride.

Today, in a similar way, God has sent His Holy Spirit with abundant provision for the bride of His Son Jesus, the Church. Included in this provision are nine beautiful spiritual gifts. By accepting these gifts, the Church is marked out as the one who is committed to become the Bride of Christ.

Nine Supernatural Gifts

These nine gifts are listed in 1 Corinthians 12:8–10. To bring out the exact meaning, I give the following literal translation:

1. A word of wisdom
2. A word of knowledge
3. Faith
4. Gifts of healings
5. Workings of miracles (literally, powers)
6. Prophecy
7. Discernings of spirits
8. Kinds of tongues
9. Interpretation of tongues

All these gifts are "manifestations." The Holy Spirit Himself is invisible, but through these gifts He manifests Himself. He makes an impact on our senses in ways that we can see or hear or feel.

All of them are "for the profit of all." Through them Christians can minister to one another. They all serve some practical purpose. They are tools, not toys.

All these gifts are supernatural. They are not the products of natural ability or special education. An illiterate person may receive a word of wisdom or of knowledge. Similarly, the gift of "faith" goes beyond the faith we all need for salvation. It is also distinct from the *fruit* of faith, which comes by a process of natural growth. It is supernatural faith that goes beyond our natural ability and produces supernatural results.

It is often suggested that these nine gifts were withdrawn at the close of the apostolic age and are not available today. But Paul thanked God for the Christians at Corinth because "you do not lack any spiritual gift as you eagerly wait for our Lord Jesus Christ to be revealed" (1 Corinthians 1:7, NIV). Obviously, therefore, Christians are expected to continue to exercise spiritual gifts until the return of Christ.

The first two gifts Paul lists—a word of wisdom and a word of knowledge—are related in a practical way. A word of knowledge gives us the facts about a situation. Then a word of wisdom shows us how God wants us to deal with that situation.

Some of the gifts are plural in both parts: for example, *gifts* of healings; *workings* of miracles; *discernings* of spirits; and *kinds* of tongues. This indicates that each healing, each miracle, each discerning, each utterance in a certain tongue (language) is a gift. If a certain gift manifests itself regularly through a certain person, we may say that the person has that gift.

Gifts That Cannot Be Earned

All these are gifts of God's grace. They are received by faith; we can never earn them or be "good enough" to exercise them.

In 1941, in the middle of the night, I had a powerful, life-changing encounter with Jesus Christ in a barrack room of the British Army. About a week later, in the same barrack room, I spoke for the first time in an unknown tongue. Then, quite unexpectedly, I went on to speak out the interpretation in beautiful, poetic English. It was an outline of God's plan for my life and ministry, which has been fulfilled, stage by stage, up to the present time (more than sixty years).

Fortunately for me, I was too "unspiritual" to know that you had to go to church to get saved, or that after speaking in a tongue you had to wait six months to receive the gift of interpretation!

From 1957 to 1961 I served as principal of a training college for African teachers in Kenya. During that time we had a sovereign visitation of the Holy Spirit in our college. In meetings with my students I saw all nine gifts of the Spirit in operation among us at various times. I also saw two of my students on different occasions actually raised from the dead. They both testified later about what they had experienced while their spirits were out of their bodies.

Later, in America, I received an unexpected gift for ministering to people who were lame. As I seated them in a chair and held their feet in my hands, the shorter leg would grow out in front of my eyes and they would be healed. Some people suggested that this was not an appropriate ministry for a dignified, scholarly Bible teacher. I decided to ask the Lord about this and felt that He gave me this answer: *I have given you a gift. There are two things you can do with it. You can use it and get more. Or you can fail to use it and lose it.*

Then and there I decided to go on using what God had given me—and, indeed, I did receive more. On occasion I have seen a short leg grow out as much as two inches. Also, the release of God's supernatural power in this way triggered other miracles. In one place, without any special prayer being offered, a man was healed of three major infirmities and delivered from nicotine addiction.

I remember one lady who came with a paper bag in her hand and a one-inch buildup on the heel of one shoe. When I took her feet in my hands, her short leg grew out a full inch. Then she opened her paper bag and took out a pair of new shoes with perfectly normal heels. They fit her perfectly.

Eventually I decided that the scriptural name for my gift was "workings of miracles" or power.

About the same time God directed me into what I came to see as a different application of the same gift. He began to use me in the public casting out of demons. Once again there were those who objected to the noisy and disorderly manifestations that often accompanied this ministry. I observed, however, that in the Gospels similar manifestations often accompanied the ministry of Jesus, so I decided to continue. In the years that followed I have seen thousands of people wonderfully delivered from demon power.

If we desire the unhindered operation of spiritual gifts, we sometimes need to set ourselves free from traditional ideas of how we should behave in church.

Another key to exercising spiritual gifts is to cultivate sensitivity to the Holy Spirit and to make room for Him to move as and when He wills.

On one occasion, while Ruth and I were having lunch with a Christian couple, the wife shared that she had a medically diagnosed genetic defect that prevented her body from utilizing certain amino acids. Her brain was progressively deteriorating.

After the husband left to keep another appointment, we walked with the wife back to their apartment. In the parking lot we paused for a moment to say goodbye. Prompted by the Holy Spirit, Ruth said, "Let me pray for you." Then we parted.

About three weeks later the husband told us that his wife had been completely healed. This was later confirmed at the same hospital where her condition had been diagnosed.

God had a place and a moment when He wanted to touch this dear woman. Ruth responded to the Holy Spirit's direction, the miracle happened and God was glorified.

Limitations of Spiritual Gifts

I feel a familiar tingle of excitement as I think back over some of the ways in which I have seen spiritual gifts manifested. At the same time it is important to understand that there are definite limits to what we can expect from spiritual gifts.

First of all, spiritual gifts are limited to the present life. Speaking of the gifts of prophecy, tongues and the word of knowledge, Paul says, "Love never fails. But where there are prophecies, they will cease; where there are tongues, they will be stilled; where there is knowledge, it will pass away. For we know in part and we prophesy in part, but when perfection comes, the imperfect disappears" (1 Corinthians 13:8–10, NIV).

We are still living in the "imperfect" age. But when we pass from time to eternity and then put on our resurrection bodies, we will no longer need the fragmentary blessings that come to us through tongues or prophecy or a word of knowledge.

The same applies to other gifts such as healings or miracles. Our resurrection bodies will never need them!

If people are excessively preoccupied with spiritual gifts, it often indicates that they are more concerned with the things of time than of eternity. Such people need to heed Paul's warning: "If only for this life we have hope in Christ, we are to be pitied more than all men" (1 Corinthians 15:19, NIV).

More important still, the exercise of spiritual gifts gives no indication of a person's character. Let me illustrate with a crude example. Suppose a person who is lazy, deceitful and conceited receives an unearned gift of a million dollars. His character will not be changed at all. He will still be lazy, deceitful and conceited. In fact, he may even be more conceited because he has a million dollars in his bank account!

The same applies to a person who receives a dramatic spiritual gift like prophecy or healings or miracles. If he was weak and unstable before, he will be just as weak and unstable afterward. But his new gift will give him greater influence with people, and he will have the added responsibility of exercising it in a way that is righteous and pleasing to God.

A major problem in the renewal has been that charismatics tend to assess ministers more by their gifts than by their character. Yet experience has demonstrated time and time again that it is possible for a person to exercise dramatic, impressive gifts yet have a defective character. Sometimes such people may even use their gifts to cover up their character imperfections.

A minister in a Scandinavian country preached on the "latter rain" of the Holy Spirit in such a powerful way that people in his congregation actually felt the Spirit falling on them like drops of rain. Yet he went straight out from those services to commit adultery. When he was charged with this, people could not believe that a man who preached like that would commit such a sin—until eventually he acknowledged it himself.

As a young preacher I greatly admired an older man who had a spectacular ministry of miracles. He also taught forcefully that it is possible for a Christian to live without sinning.

Yet eventually he divorced his wife, married his secretary and died an alcoholic. Other well known and successful preachers have experienced similar personal tragedies.

When confronted with cases such as these, people often respond, "But surely if a person misuses one of these gifts, God will take it away."

Yet the answer is no! The gifts of the Spirit are exactly what the name implies—genuine gifts, not loans with conditions or a repayment schedule attached. "For the gifts and the calling of God are irrevocable" (Romans 11:29). Once we receive one of these gifts, we are free to use it, misuse it or just not use it at all. Ultimately, however, God will require an account of what we have done or not done. We need to bear always in mind the warning of Jesus: "You will know them by their fruits" (Matthew 7:20, NASB)—not by their gifts.

Jesus followed up these words by an explicit warning that the exercise of spiritual gifts is not necessarily a passport to heaven:

> "Not everyone who says to Me, 'Lord, Lord,' shall enter the kingdom of heaven, but he who does the will of My Father in heaven. Many will say to Me in that day, 'Lord, Lord, have we not prophesied in Your name, cast out demons in Your name, and done many wonders in Your name?' And then I will declare to them, 'I never knew you; depart from Me, you who practice lawlessness!'"
>
> Matthew 7:21–23

This indicates that it is possible for a person to exercise spiritual gifts and at the same time to "practice lawlessness." What is lawlessness? It is an arrogant assumption that God's moral and ethical standards no longer apply to those who can exercise gifts of supernatural power.

Obviously such ministries may at times confront us with the need to make difficult personal decisions. How should we respond?

First we must keep in mind Paul's warning to Timothy: "Do not . . . share in other people's sins; keep yourself pure" (1 Timothy 5:22).

Second, we must keep in mind the warning Jesus gave us concerning such unethical ministries: "Not everyone who says to Me, 'Lord, Lord,' shall enter the kingdom of heaven" (Matthew 7:21).

We each need to ask ourselves: *What is the will of God in my life? What does my Father expect of me?*

For my part, I feel that God has given me a clear, simple answer: "This is the will of God, your sanctification" (1 Thessalonians 4:3)—meaning that we should be holy. To this the Holy Spirit has added a warning: "Without holiness no one will see the Lord" (Hebrews 12:14, NIV). It is my determination, then, to pursue holiness.

In the next chapter I will deal with the opposite side of the coin: the fruit of the Holy Spirit.

fourteen

THE FRUIT OF THE SPIRIT

MY PREVIOUS CHAPTER focused on the *gifts* of the Holy Spirit. The focus of this chapter will be the *fruit* of the Spirit.

There is a difference in kind between gifts and fruit. This may be illustrated by comparing a Christmas tree with an apple tree. A Christmas tree carries gifts. Each gift is attached to it by a single act and received from it by a single act: receiving. The gift is not earned or labored for; no time or effort is required of the person receiving the gift.

Both time and hard work, on the other hand, are required to cultivate an apple tree. To produce fruit it must go through a series of stages taking several years. First the seed must be placed in the earth. From this a root goes down into the soil, and at the same time a sprout rises upward. Over a period of years the sprout grows into a tree. In due course blossoms appear on the tree. Then these fall off and fruit begins to develop.

But if the tree is to become strong, the blossoms or young fruit must be plucked off in the first years so the root system will develop to support a strong tree. Several years must pass before the apples are fit to eat. (Under the Law of Moses at least four years were required; see Leviticus 19:23–25.)

At various stages in its growth, an apple tree is very fragile. Strong winds may uproot the young tree; at a later stage frost may destroy either the blossoms or the fruit. In this process seed and fruit are inseparably linked to each other. Fruit must grow from a seed, but it takes fruit to produce further seeds. At the beginning of creation God ordained that every "fruit tree [should yield] fruit according to its kind, whose seed is in itself" (Genesis 1:11).

This establishes an important spiritual principle: Christians who do not produce spiritual fruit in their own lives have no seed to sow into the lives of others.

The New Testament speaks of spiritual *gifts* in the plural. The nine gifts are listed in 1 Corinthians 12:8–10. The New Testament speaks of spiritual *fruit,* on the other hand, in the singular. The nine forms of spiritual fruit are listed in Galatians 5:22–23: love, joy, peace, longsuffering (patience), kindness, goodness, faithfulness, gentleness, self-control.

Love—the primary form of fruit—is listed first. The others that follow may be understood as different ways in which the fruit of love manifests itself:

> Joy is love rejoicing.
> Peace is love resting.
> Longsuffering is love forbearing.
> Kindness is love serving others.
> Goodness is love seeking the best for others.
> Faithfulness is love keeping its promises.
> Gentleness is love ministering to the hurts of others.
> Self-control is love in control.

We could also describe the fruit of the Spirit as different ways in which the character of Jesus manifests itself through those He indwells. When all the forms of fruit are fully developed, it is as if Jesus by the Holy Spirit is incarnated in His disciple.

Seven Stages of Spiritual Development

In 2 Peter 1:5–7 the apostle lists seven successive stages in the development of a fully formed Christian character:

> For this very reason, giving all diligence, add to your faith virtue, to virtue knowledge, to knowledge self-control, to self-control perseverance, to perseverance godliness, to godliness brotherly kindness, and to brotherly kindness love.

Peter begins by warning us that to go through this process successfully will demand *diligence.* Paul expresses the same thing in another way: "The *hardworking* farmer must be first to partake of the crops" (2 Timothy 2:6, emphasis added). There can be no real success in developing Christian character without diligence, or hard work.

The process Peter describes could be compared to that by which an apple seed develops into a mature apple. The seed is God's Word implanted in the heart. This produces faith, which is the indispensable starting point. Then out of faith there follow seven successive stages of development.

Stage 1: Virtue

Stage 1 is variously translated *virtue* (2 Peter 1:5) or *moral excellence* (2 Peter 1:5, NASB). In secular Greek the word was applied to excellence in any area of life—molding a clay pot, steering a boat, playing a flute. Here, too, in the New Testament, I believe, its meaning should not be restricted to moral character. It covers every possible area of life.

A teacher who comes to Christ should become an excellent teacher. A nurse should become an excellent nurse. A Christian businessman should excel in his field of business. There is no room for sloppiness or laziness in any area of the Christian life. Rarely if ever does God call a person out of failure in a secular calling to success in a spiritual calling. He who is unfaithful in the least—the secular—will be unfaithful also in the greatest—the spiritual (see Luke 16:10).

Stage 2: Knowledge

Stage 2 of spiritual development is *knowledge.* There are, of course, many different forms of knowledge. The knowledge extolled in Scripture is primarily practical, not merely theoretical. It is knowledge that works. Coming to Christ out of a background of speculative philosophy, I was impressed by this most of all about the Bible. It was so intensely practical!

The scriptural example is the teaching of Jesus Himself. It did not come under the category of what we would call theology. He never propounded complicated, abstract theories. His teaching was based on familiar, practical activities: sowing seed, catching fish, caring for livestock.

The most essential form of knowledge in the Christian life is the knowledge of God's will as revealed in Scripture. This, too, is practical. It demands a regular, systematic study of the whole Bible. "All Scripture is given by inspiration of God, and is profitable for doctrine, for reproof, for correction, for instruction in righteousness, that the man of God may be complete, thoroughly equipped for every good work" (2 Timothy 3:16–17).

I have been shocked to discover how many people who claim to be serious Christians have never once read through the entire Bible. Such people set limits of their own regarding their spiritual development.

Stage 3: Self-Control

After knowledge comes *self-control,* also called *self-discipline* (2 Timothy 1:7, NIV). This is the stage at which a Christian must prove himself a genuine *disciple*—a person under *discipline*—and not merely a church member.

This kind of discipline must be applied in every major area of our personality—our emotions, our attitudes, our appetites, our thought life. It must govern not only our actions but, more importantly, our reactions.

Stage 4: Perseverance

Until we have developed this kind of discipline, we cannot move up to the next stage, *perseverance,* which implies the ability to overcome the various tests and trials that will inevitably expose any weak, undisciplined areas of our personality. That pinpoints one major reason some Christians never progress beyond a certain stage of spiritual development. They never fulfill these two requirements of *self-control* and *endurance.* To take an illustration from the apple tree, their blossoms are blown away by the winds of adversity or their young fruit is killed by the frost of rejection.

Stage 5: Godliness

In the three remaining stages of development, the beauty of a truly Christian character unfolds. *Godliness* is the mark of a person whose life is centered in God—a person who has become a vessel of the presence of God. Wherever such a person goes, the atmosphere is permeated by a faint but unique and pervasive fragrance. There may not be any preaching or other religious activity. Yet people become strangely aware of eternal issues.

The late British evangelist Smith Wigglesworth relates an incident illustrating the impact that a godly presence can have in a non-religious atmosphere. After some moments of private prayer, Smith took his seat in a railway car. Without a word spoken, the man in the opposite seat, a complete stranger, blurted out, "Your presence convicts me of sin." Smith was then able to introduce him to Christ.

Stage 6: Brotherly Kindness

The last two stages of development depict two different kinds of love. The first, *brotherly kindness,* describes the way disciples of Jesus Christ should relate to their brothers and sisters in the Lord.

When I first began to consider this list of the seven stages of spiritual development, it surprised me that brotherly kindness—the kind of love that Christians should have for one another—should be the last stage but one. But then I realized that the Bible is very realistic. It does not paint a sentimental, religious picture of the way we as Christians relate to one another. Let me say something that may shock you, that is based on sixty years of close association with Christians of many different backgrounds: *It is not easy for Christians to love one another!*

This is amply confirmed by two thousand years of Church history. Scarcely a century has passed that has not been marked by bitter strife and contention—and even open hatred—between rival groups of Christians, all of whom often claimed to be "the true Church."

The fact that a person has repented of his sins and claimed salvation in Christ does not mean his whole character has been instantly transformed. Certainly a vitally important process of change has been set in motion, but it may take many years for that change to be worked out in every area of that person's character.

When David needed stones to fit into his sling to slay Goliath, he went down to the valley—the lowly place of humility. There in the brook he found the "five smooth stones" he needed (1 Samuel 17:40). What had made them smooth? Two pressures: first, the water flowing over them; second, their continual jostling against one another.

That is a picture of how Christian character is formed. First there is the continual "washing of water by the word" (Ephesians 5:26). Second, as the stones jostle one another in personal relationships, the rough edges are gradually worn down until they become smooth.

In parentheses, let me add that when Jesus needs living stones for His sling, He, like David, goes to the valley—the place of humility. There He chooses stones that have been made smooth by the action of God's Word and by the pressures of regular fellowship with other believers.

It is a mark of spiritual maturity to sincerely love our fellow Christians, not simply for what they are in themselves, but for what they mean to Jesus, who shed His lifeblood for each of them.

Stage 7: Love

The final stage of development, *agape love,* represents the full, ripe fruit of Christian character. This is no longer how we relate only to our fellow believers. It is God's own love for the unthankful and the unholy. It is the love that causes us to "bless those who curse [us], do good to those who hate [us], and pray for those who spitefully use [us] and persecute [us]" (Matthew 5:44).

It is the love Christ demonstrated on the cross when He prayed for those who crucified Him, "Father, forgive them, for they do not know what they do" (Luke 23:34). It was the same love that caused Stephen to pray for those who were stoning him, "Lord, do not charge them with this sin" (Acts 7:60). It is the love that changed Saul the persecutor into Paul the servant of Christ, who became "all things to all men, that [he] might by all means save some" (1 Corinthians 9:22).

For my part, when I contemplate the Bible's picture of the fully developed fruit of the Holy Spirit, I am both humbled and inspired. Humbled, because I still have so far to go. Inspired, because I have caught a glimpse of something more beautiful than anything this world has to offer.

I echo the words of Paul: "I do not count myself to have apprehended; but one thing I do, forgetting those things which are behind and reaching forward to those things which are ahead, I press toward the goal for the prize of the upward call of God in Christ Jesus" (Philippians 3:13–14).

PART 4

LIFE'S
BITTER POOL

IN SPEAKING TO LARGE and small congregations at different times, I have often asked people, "How many of you have had to struggle with disappointment?" Very few people in such a congregation would ever say they have never confronted disappointment. It is one of the things that comes our way.

I would like for you to understand and learn how to face disappointments and get the best out of them.

The story of the bitter pool goes back three thousand years, but the truths it contains are as vivid and real today as in the time of Moses. We will look together at some of these truths to see how they apply to our own lives and situations.

fifteen

LESSONS FROM THE POOL

WE CAN LEARN valuable lessons from an incident that occurred in the history of God's people, Israel, just after they had been miraculously delivered out of Egypt and had passed through the waters of the Red Sea. First we will look at the climax of their miraculous deliverance in Exodus 15 (NIV here and throughout part 4, except where noted):

> When Pharaoh's horses, chariots and horsemen went into the sea, the LORD brought the waters of the sea back over them, but the Israelites walked through the sea on dry ground. Then Miriam the prophetess, Aaron's sister, took a tambourine in her hand, and all the women followed her, with tambourines and dancing. Miriam sang to them:
>
> > "Sing to the LORD,
> >   for he is highly exalted.
> > The horse and its rider
> >   he has hurled into the sea."
> >   Exodus 15:19–21

107

That was a tremendous triumph, wasn't it? Israel had passed through the waters of the Red Sea miraculously as if on dry ground. Then, when their enemy followed them in, God brought the waters back over the Egyptians, sweeping them away and putting an end to the entire force pursuing His people. Not one Egyptian survived.

I am sure the Israelites concluded that now all their troubles were over and that the rest of their journey to the Promised Land would be easy and uneventful. As a result they were unprepared for what lay ahead. This is what followed after this tremendous deliverance:

> Then Moses led Israel from the Red Sea and they went into the Desert of Shur. For three days they traveled in the desert without finding water. When they came to Marah, they could not drink its water because it was bitter. (That is why the place is called Marah.) So the people grumbled against Moses, saying, "What are we to drink?"
>
> Exodus 15:22–24

Picture that scene for a moment: They had experienced a glorious deliverance. They were triumphant, exulting, feeling that everything was under God's control. Then they were led by God through Moses into the wilderness of Shur, where they went three days without finding water. They had an emergency supply of water with them in water skins, of course, but they must have been running low. The children and cattle were beginning to become thirsty; they were all weary with the hot and dusty journey.

Then in the distance they saw the gleam of water. Some of them must have started to run to get there to quench their thirst. Oh, what a bitter disappointment when they stooped down to drink! The waters were so bitter in this pool called Marah (Hebrew for "bitter") that they could not drink.

The people were unprepared for this situation. They could not conceive that such a thing would happen to them when

God was actually leading them and when He had just granted them such a tremendous deliverance and victory.

One person was not unprepared, however, and that was God. Let me tell you, no matter how many times we may feel unprepared, God is never unprepared. God never has an emergency. God is never confronted with a situation for which He has no answer.

Faith Releases God's Power

Scholars estimate that there were probably around three million Israelites there. Think of the noise of three million people all grumbling at one time! But while the people grumbled, one man, Moses, had the sense to pray. I am sure it must have been hard for Moses to hear his own voice. But this is what followed:

> Then Moses cried out to the LORD, and the LORD showed him a piece of wood. He threw it into the water, and the water became sweet.
>
> There the LORD made a decree and a law for them, and there he tested them. He said, "If you listen carefully to the voice of the LORD your God and do what is right in his eyes, if you pay attention to his commands and keep all his decrees, I will not bring on you any of the diseases I brought on the Egyptians, for I am the LORD, who heals you."
>
> Exodus 15:25–26

In the Hebrew language, the same word is used for a tree while it is growing and for a tree that has been cut down, when it becomes a long plank or beam. The text does not indicate whether the tree was growing and Moses had to cut it down or whether it was a tree that had fallen. But whatever it was, it was the key to the situation. When Moses picked up that wood and threw it into the water, the water became sweet.

It is important to see that the Scripture does not say the tree made the water sweet. There was nothing magical about the wood. It was the supernatural power of God that made the water sweet. The casting in of the tree was the act of faith that released the miracle-working power of God into the water. That is how God's power is usually released in our lives: It takes a specific act of faith to release it. The act of faith is the key that unlocks the miracle-working power of God and makes it available in the situation where we need it.

This principle is illustrated many times, further on in the Old Testament, in the ministry of the prophet Elisha. There was a stream near Jericho, for instance, of which the waters were bad. The people could not drink it, and it made the ground infertile. Elisha took some salt, threw it into the water and said, "This is what the LORD says: 'I have healed this water'" (2 Kings 2:21). The water was healed not by the salt but by the supernatural power of God. Casting the salt into the water released God's power. Interestingly enough, you can go to Jericho today and still see what they call Elisha's Stream flowing pure and fresh. That miracle had a long-lasting effect!

In another situation, Elisha was confronted by some food that had been poisoned (see 2 Kings 4:38–41). The people were about to suffer, perhaps even die. Elisha took some flour, threw it into the pot and said, in effect, "The pot is healed." It was not the flour that counteracted the poison, but the supernatural power of God released by that act of faith.

And so it was with these bitter waters. The act of Moses throwing in the tree released the power of God that turned the bitter waters sweet. God had that tree ready; He knew what had to be done. But it was only through prayer that Moses could find the solution. His act of faith was the key that unlocked the miracle-working power of God.

Lessons from the Bitter Pool

Two lessons stand out for me from this story of the bitter pool. The first lesson is, *Great victories prepare us for great testings.* The fact that God has given you a tremendous deliverance—a victory, blessing, healing or whatever—does not mean the rest of your life will be without further testing. Rather, a tremendous deliverance means we will be better equipped for the next test. In fact, the greater the victory, the greater the test you are able to face on the basis of that victory. That was the Israelites' mistake. They probably thought that just because they had had a tremendous deliverance, nothing else could happen that would challenge their faith. Consequently they were not ready when they came to the bitter pool. Instead of praying, they grumbled.

The second lesson—and this is vital—is, *The bitter pool was in God's program.* God actually led them to that pool, and He had a purpose in bringing them there. This is true in our lives as well. From time to time God permits us to be confronted with a bitter pool. *He has a purpose.*

Let me give you a few contemporary examples of the kind of bitter pool you and I may have to face. The first example I think of is a broken marriage. Alas, how many people today have had to face the bitter pool of a marriage that has ended in divorce. This leaves deep wounds in the human personality—bitterness, agony, embarrassment.

Another bitter pool is business failure. Perhaps you have worked for years to build up some kind of business and establish yourself financially. Then, through circumstances you cannot control (a change in the economy, for instance), you find yourself penniless, maybe quite well on in life. That is a bitter pool.

Another bitter pool is disillusionment with a human leader. It may be a religious or political leader or even a parent. You may have followed this person, given him or her your best in service.

111

The person in whom you had confidence, whom you looked up to, was one day not what he seemed. Suddenly he or she had feet of clay; he failed you. Your confidence was misplaced.

Or you may have suffered a health breakdown, a physical breakdown or, worse still, a mental or emotional breakdown. Now you are trying to put together the broken pieces of a life that was strong and healthy and victorious.

I would like to ask you a question: Are you willing to learn the lessons God has for you in the bitter pool?

sixteen

∞

THE PURPOSE OF TESTING

I WILL MAKE a further application from the story of the bitter pool in this chapter and address the purpose of testing. The question in our lives, you see, is not whether we will experience testing, but only *how we will respond to the testing.* The testing at Marah exposed an area in the character of the Israelites that needed to be dealt with—an area that was expressed in grumbling.

Let me tell you this: The Bible has nothing good to say about grumbling! Grumbling is a way not to solve your problems but to magnify them. You will never find the way out of your problems by grumbling.

If, when you come under pressure, you begin to grumble, then you are like the Israelites: There is an area in your character that needs to be dealt with. God has known that area was there all along, but He had to let you come to the bitter pool so you could find out what was really inside you. Actually, the act of grumbling indicates a lack of faith, a lack of gratitude, self-centeredness—many serious problems that hinder our progress in the Lord.

God had a lot farther for Israel to go than the pool of Marah; He was taking them to the Promised Land. But they were not fit to make the full journey until that thing in their character, which was exposed at Marah, had been dealt with. So when you come to *your* Marah, your bitter waters, and you begin to grumble, realize that there is something in you that must be dealt with; and that God has brought you to this place so He might deal with that thing. But He can deal with it only if you cooperate.

The Bible warns us clearly and in many places that we are going to experience testing. Here is one particularly clear passage:

> Consider it pure joy, my brothers, whenever you face trials of many kinds. . . .
>
> James 1:2

I never read those words without asking myself, *Is that how I react to trials of many kinds?* Is that how you react to trials of many kinds? When you are walking with the Lord and are confronted with a trial, do you consider it pure joy? Do you say, "Hallelujah! Praise God for this trial"? Or do you do what the Israelites did—begin to grumble, "Lord, why did You let this happen? God, I thought You had this situation under control! Now I don't know what to do."

James continues:

> . . . Because you know that the testing of your faith develops perseverance. Perseverance must finish its work so that you may be mature and complete, not lacking anything.
>
> verses 3–4

One essential element in Christian character is perseverance. Until we achieve perseverance, there are goals in God we can never attain. Perseverance is brought out by the testing of our faith. There is really only one way to learn perseverance, and that is by persevering. In order to persevere, you have to be in a situation in which perseverance is needed.

"Perseverance must finish its work," James says, "so that you may be mature and complete, not lacking anything." That is God's goal for you: to be mature, fully grown up, complete, having a fully rounded Christian character, not lacking anything. Do you want that? Do you want to be mature and complete, lacking nothing? How could you wish for anything else?

If you do want this, you have to go through the process, and the process may include your particular Marah or bitter pool. There is a bitter pool somewhere in the life of nearly every one of us, a place of bitter disappointment where something that gleams and shines and seems beautiful is not really what we thought it would be.

When encountering a bitter pool, there are just two alternative responses. The people grumbled; that was the response of unbelief. Moses prayed; that was the response of faith. The people who grumbled got nothing; the man who prayed got the answer. Which will you choose? The next time you come to a bitter pool, which are you going to do?

On the shore of that pool, Moses prayed and cried out to the Lord. There was no other source of help. And when Moses took that course—to pray rather than to grumble; to choose faith rather than to choose unbelief—God responded with a new revelation of Himself.

That was God's purpose in bringing Israel to the bitter pool—to bring His people to the place where they could receive the revelation He had for them. He had something for them to learn, and He set them in a situation in which the revelation He had for them would be appropriate. The Lord responded with a revelation of Himself.

It was a double revelation (which I will deal with more fully in the next two chapters). First He revealed to them the tree—the means of healing. Second, and more important still, He revealed to them a new aspect of Himself, the Lord their Healer. That was His ultimate objective in their experience at the bitter pool.

I want to point out a principle that has been summed up very succinctly in a statement I heard somebody make once. Actually, I did not like the statement when I heard it the first time because I thought, *This doesn't suggest that life is going to be the way I'd like it to be!* The statement is this: *Man's disappointments are God's appointments.*

As I stated previously, disappointment is one of the things that nearly all of us face. Disappointment really is a bitter pool. When your hopes are set high, you are moving forward and everything seems to be going right. Then it all falls apart and crumbles; you are left with nothing but disappointed hopes. That is a bitter pool.

But what I want you to grasp is this: God has led you to that bitter pool. He has something good for you at the bitter pool if you respond the right way. Man's disappointments are God's appointments.

It has something to do with human nature. When everything is going well and life is pretty easy, most of us tend to be somewhat superficial. We are content with the status quo, content to go to church and pay our tithes and say our prayers and lead a fairly respectable kind of life. But God has something much further and much deeper for us. Somehow or another He gets us to the bitter pool. Then, in the depths of agony and disappointment, we cry out as Moses did. When we do, we get a much deeper and fuller revelation of God, which comes only on the shores of the bitter pool.

If you have faced a bitter pool in the past or if you are facing one now, bear in mind that "my disappointment is God's appointment."

Now we will look at the revelation God had for His people at the bitter pool.

seventeen

The Healing Tree

THERE WERE TWO ASPECTS of God's revelation to the Israelites at the bitter pool at Marah. The first was the revelation of the healing tree; the second was the revelation of God the Healer.

We will start by looking back at the verse in Exodus 15 that speaks about Moses and that tree:

> Then he cried out to the LORD, and the LORD showed him a tree; and he threw it into the waters, and the waters became sweet.
>
> Exodus 15:25, NASB

The solution to the problem was found in that tree. And that tree speaks of one of the main themes in the entire Bible. It speaks of another tree that was raised, perhaps 2,400 years later, on a hill called Golgotha: the cross. Whenever you read in the Bible about a tree, be alert to see if it is really a reference to the cross of Jesus.

117

We need to understand the Hebrew use of the word *tree,* which I touched on in chapter 15. We saw that in the Hebrew language, the word for "tree" is used for a tree when it is growing, and it is still used for a tree after it has been cut down. Even a long pole or some such thing is still referred to as a tree.

A tree can also be a gibbet, a gallows or a cross. There are several examples of this; we will look at a few of them. First of all, in the book of Deuteronomy:

If a man guilty of a capital offense is put to death and his body is hung on a tree, you must not leave his body on the tree overnight. Be sure to bury him that same day, because anyone who is hung on a tree is under God's curse.

Deuteronomy 21:22–23

That way of executing a person was often followed in the Old Testament. Sometimes he was killed first and then hung on the tree, and sometimes he was killed by hanging him on the tree. But the Law of Moses stated that no man must ever be left hanging on a tree overnight because "anyone who is hung on a tree is under God's curse."

You will remember in the record of the crucifixion that after Jesus died on the cross, the Jewish religious leaders went to Pontius Pilate and asked him if the body might be taken down. They did not want it to remain there, as a display of the curse, over the following holy day.

Paul took this ordinance in the book of Deuteronomy and used it in the epistle to the Galatians to interpret the full significance of the death of Jesus on the cross:

Christ redeemed us from the curse of the law by becoming a curse for us, for it is written: "Cursed is everyone who is hung on a tree." He redeemed us in order that the blessing given to Abraham might come to the Gentiles through Christ Jesus, so that by faith we might receive the promise of the Spirit.

Galatians 3:13–14

Paul was citing the passage in Deuteronomy that I just quoted. In God's purpose of redemption (as we saw in chapter 7) Jesus was permitted to become a curse. He took the curse that was due to a lost, fallen race that He might redeem us from the curse. Those in the first century who knew the Word of God from the Old Testament knew that in that act Jesus, in the purpose of God, *became* a curse that we might inherit the blessing. The evidence that Jesus became a curse for us was that He was hung on the tree.

That part of the divine exchange—Jesus became the curse that we might receive the blessing—is like the waters of Marah. Moses casting the tree into the pool is a pattern or picture of you and me taking what was accomplished on our behalf on the cross and using it to make our bitter pool sweet. When you think of the tree that was cast into the water, think of the cross of Jesus and the fact that, on that cross, Jesus took the bitterness of the curse that we might have the sweetness of the blessing. Jesus took the bitter water that we might be able to drink the sweet.

Peter, too, refers to the cross as a tree, speaking of Jesus, and brings the same truth out:

> He himself bore our sins in his body on the tree, so that we might die to sins and live for righteousness; by his wounds you have been healed.
>
> 1 Peter 2:24

Recall two other parts of the divine exchange: Jesus became sin that we might receive His righteousness; He was wounded that we might be healed. All this is brought out in the use of the word *tree* for the cross. It was on that tree that full healing was obtained for the whole human race—spiritual healing from sin, physical healing from sickness, deliverance from the curse, the right to inherit the blessing. On the cross every human need was met by the substitutionary, atoning, sacrificial death of Jesus Christ. That is the healing tree—the revelation of what was accomplished for you and me by the death of Jesus on the tree, which was the cross.

As you picture in your mind Moses casting the tree into the bitter water, that it might be made sweet, picture yourself taking the truth of the cross, applying it in your life and turning your own bitter pool into sweetness.

The healing and deliverance that come from the tree, the cross of Jesus, must be applied in our lives by an act of faith. Just as Moses, by an act of faith, threw that wood into the bitter water, so we, too, must exercise faith when we confront our bitter pool. We must have faith in what Jesus accomplished on the cross and, metaphorically, take that tree and throw it into our bitter pool. It requires an act of faith to release the miracle-working power that is in the cross of Jesus Christ—power to make the bitter water sweet.

I want to suggest to you four simple, practical steps you can take to change that bitter pool into sweet.

First, recognize that the bitter pool is in God's program. God led you there, He knows all about it and He has the remedy.

Second, let God deal with any defects in your character that have been exposed by the bitter pool. If you have grumbled when you should have prayed, bear in mind there is something in you that must be dealt with by the Holy Spirit.

Third, accept by faith what Jesus did for you on the cross. "He himself bore our sins in his body on the tree, so that we might die to sins and live for righteousness; by his wounds you have been healed." It is not *You will be healed* but *You have been healed.* As far as God is concerned, it is already done, finished, accomplished!

Here is the fourth and vital step: Begin to thank God for what Jesus has done on your behalf. Begin to receive by thanking Him for whatever it is you need—forgiveness, healing (whether emotional or physical), release from resentment, bitterness, rebellion, confusion. Thanking God in faith corresponds to throwing the tree into the water. The purest expression of faith that you and I are capable of is simply thanking

God—without seeing any change or waiting for the evidence, but believing what God says about the cross of Jesus. We can then begin to thank Him for what Jesus did on our behalf on the cross. Thanking Him releases that miracle-working power to change the bitter water to sweet.

eighteen

The Lord Our Healer

In this chapter we will look at the second aspect of God's revelation to the Israelites at the bitter pool at Marah: the revelation of Him as our Healer.

In every spiritual experience, whenever we receive provision from God, we need to look beyond the provision to the Provider. The provision for the Israelites was the tree, but the Provider was the Lord. The Lord did not allow Israel merely to receive the revelation of the tree. The revelation of the tree led to the revelation of the Lord as their Healer. Again from Exodus 15:25–26:

> Then he [Moses] cried out to the Lord, and the Lord showed him a tree; and he threw it into the waters, and the waters became sweet. There He made for them a statute and regulation, and there He tested them. And He said, "If you will give earnest heed to the voice of the Lord your God, and do what is right in His sight, and give ear to His commandments, and keep all His statutes, I will put none of the diseases on

you which I have put on the Egyptians; for I, the LORD, am
your healer [or I am the LORD your healer]."

NASB

The ultimate revelation was not a revelation of a provision,
but a revelation of the Provider. That is a very important principle to lay hold of. Every revelation of God, if we follow it
through to its intended conclusion, will bring us to God Himself. "I am the LORD your healer."

The word translated "healer" is the modern Hebrew word
for a doctor. It has not changed in more than three thousand
years. The Lord wants to be His people's doctor, their physician. It was that revelation for which He was preparing His
people when He brought them to the pool.

A revelation is not something the natural mind can receive.
Normally we have to land in a situation in which we need that
revelation.

Many years ago I lay for one whole year in a hospital with
a condition that the doctors were unable to heal. In that situation, through the Bible and through the Holy Spirit, the Lord
revealed Himself to me as my doctor, my physician. "I am the
LORD your healer." That is the revelation to which He is bringing all of us.

One thing we must understand is that God never changes.
He not only *was* His people's doctor; He *is* His people's doctor. Malachi 3:6, right at the end of the Old Covenant, says:
"I the LORD do not change." (Or, "I am the LORD, I do not
change.") He was, He is and He will be. He does not change.

Then, in the New Testament: "Jesus Christ is the same yesterday and today and forever" (Hebrews 13:8). Often we can
believe for yesterday and for forever, but what about today?
We can believe something happened in the Bible and that it
will happen when we get to heaven, but let's not forget, it is
for today, too! *Today* Jesus Christ is the same as He was when
He was on earth. *Today* God is the same as He was at the bitter pool. He is our physician, our doctor, our healer.

123

One verse in the New Testament describes the ministry of Jesus on earth more completely than anywhere else I know. Peter was describing to the household of Cornelius the ministry of Jesus on earth as he himself witnessed it:

> ". . . God anointed Jesus of Nazareth with the Holy Spirit and power, and . . . he went around doing good and healing all who were under the power of the devil, because God was with him."
> Acts 10:38

In this verse we have all three Persons of the eternal Godhead. God the Father anointed Jesus the Son with the Holy Spirit. What was the result? Healing, liberation, deliverance and wholeness for everybody Jesus came in contact with. It seems to me, if I can say it reverently, that there is almost a jealousy among the persons of the Godhead when it comes to blessing the human race. Not one of them wants to be left out. The Father anointed the Son with the Spirit, that all of them might share in this ministry of mercy and deliverance and making people whole.

This is the revelation of God's eternal nature. God had allowed His people to come to a place of need at the waters of Marah so that they might receive this revelation of Him.

Today, if you are in a place of need and faced with those bitter waters, I want to suggest that you take this attitude: "God permitted this. God is in this. He has a program. I won't grumble, I'll pray. I'll wait on God and allow Him to speak to me. I'll let Him show me the revelation He has for me in this situation."

The full purpose of God, you see, is not merely to reveal the tree, but to reveal Himself. This needs to be said to multitudes of Christians today. God never intends us to stop short at an experience, a doctrine, a revelation or a blessing. We thank God for every one of these things, but we cannot rest in them. Each one of them is, in a sense, impersonal and impermanent. What we need, in the last resort, is a person. And every true doctrine or revelation we receive will always lead us in the end to the Person of God Himself.

Follow me in a few Scriptures from the Old and New Testaments that bring out this principle.

In Exodus 19:4 God said to Israel, "You yourselves have seen what I did to Egypt, and how I carried you on eagles' wings and . brought you to myself." Notice that the purpose of God was to bring Israel to Himself—not just to the Law, not just to a covenant, not just to the Promised Land, but to Himself. That is always God's purpose.

In Psalm 73:26 the psalmist writes, "My flesh and my heart may fail, but God is the strength of my heart and my portion forever." My portion is not some blessing or experience or revelation; my portion is God Himself. I will not settle for anything less.

Isaiah 12:2: "Surely God is my salvation; I will trust and not be afraid. The LORD, the LORD, is my strength and my song; he has become my salvation." That is a revelation! When you can say, "The Lord is my salvation"—not the church, not a doctrine, not an experience, but the Lord—there you will be secure. There you will have come to the fullness of the revelation.

And then those beautiful words of Jesus in Matthew 11:28: "Come to me, all you who are weary and burdened, and I will give you rest." This is the ultimate invitation. Don't stop short at anything less than God manifested in Jesus Christ. Come to Him. He will give you rest. The human heart can never be satisfied with something impersonal. Ultimately we need a person, and God is the Person that every one of us must come to know.

So don't stop short at the tree. Don't stop short at the experience. No matter how blessed these may be, always move on to the revelation of the Lord Himself.

nineteen

∞

DEATH BEFORE RESURRECTION

IN THIS CHAPTER I will express a vital truth of our experience as a comprehensive principle that operates in every area of life. In fact, God has built this principle into the operation of the very universe itself: *Death comes before resurrection.*

Two passages of Scripture in particular state this principle. The first, found in Hosea, is a prophetic passage that I believe is coming into fulfillment in our day. It is the promise of God to His people, Israel, to restore them—to Himself, to the blessings He has for them, and to their land. He actually describes the way He will work out their restoration. Read carefully because, as so often happens, the way God does things is not the way you and I would expect. We must watch, therefore, or we will miss what God is doing. The Lord says:

"Therefore I am now going to allure her;
    I will lead her into the desert
    and speak tenderly to her."

Hosea 2:14

The word *allure* is a mystical word. It contains the thought of God's dealing with us in a way that draws us and yet that we do not fully understand. But He also says, "I will lead her into the desert"—not normally the place of blessing!—"and speak tenderly to her."

This is a beautiful expression in Hebrew. Literally the Lord says, "I will speak to her heart." But it is not always possible for God to speak to our hearts. Sometimes our hearts are closed. Sometimes we are not responsive. So God has to work in our lives to bring about situations (such as bringing Israel into the desert) in which He can speak to our hearts.

This is what God says once He has gained Israel's attention:

"There I will give her back her vineyards,
    and will make the Valley of Achor a door of hope.
There she will sing as in the days of her youth,
    as in the day she came up out of Egypt."

verse 15

In Hebrew the word *Achor* means "trouble." God is saying He will make the Valley of Trouble a door of hope. (The phrase *door of hope* in Hebrew is *Petah Tikva.* It is the name of one of the major suburbs of Tel Aviv today and is taken from this passage.)

We saw early in this section that Miriam and all the women of Israel sang praises right on the shores of the Red Sea. In Hosea God says, "I'm going to give her back a song." Maybe you have lost *your* song. It is tragic when this happens to a Christian. Perhaps you used to have a song in your heart and praised the Lord freely and spontaneously; but now you feel

127

heaviness, doubt or a sense of being left out. God wants to give you back your song.

At this point we come to the purpose of God—His revelation. Just as at the bitter pool, God wants to give a revelation of Himself:

> "In that day," declares the LORD,
>   "you will call me 'my husband';
>   you will no longer call me 'my master.'"
>
> verse 16

Israel's relationship to the Lord under the Old Covenant was a marriage relationship, but they knew Him as Baal, Master. The relationship was not really based on heart commitment or on deep personal love. God's purpose in dealing with Israel was to bring her to a new revelation of Himself. And God promises that when He restores you, you will come back on a higher level of revelation. You will not just call Him *Master,* but you will call Him *Husband*—an intimate word in Hebrew. What God is saying, in effect, is, "I'll show you Myself in a new light, as the One who loves you as a husband loves his wife." What a revelation of love and of deep tenderness!

When I observe all the infinite wisdom and patience God has expended—and is still expending—in dealing with Israel, I take tremendous courage in my own life. If God is so patient with Israel, then He can be that patient with me. Even if I must go through the Valley of Trouble, if I continue and persevere, not giving up or turning back, not grumbling or starting to complain, then the Valley of Trouble will become for me, as for Israel, a door of hope. That door will lead me to a new and deeper and fuller revelation of the Lord, to a revelation of His love and compassion and tenderness.

Sometimes it is only in seasons of grief that we can really appreciate compassion and tenderness. If you are facing a bitter pool, bear in mind that out of that pool God will reveal Himself to you, if you will let Him speak to your heart.

Now I want to illustrate the same principle of God's dealing from a passage in the New Testament. Paul is writing in a personal vein about very difficult experiences he has gone through:

> We do not want you to be uninformed, brothers, about the hardships we suffered in the province of Asia. We were under great pressure, far beyond our ability to endure, so that we despaired even of life. Indeed, in our hearts we felt the sentence of death. But this happened that we might not rely on ourselves but on God, who raises the dead. He has delivered us from such deadly peril [literally, *from such a death*], and he will deliver us. On him we have set our hope that he will continue to deliver us.
>
> 2 Corinthians 1:8–10

Here is a man speaking out of personal experience. The pressure, he said, was "far beyond our ability to endure" and that "we despaired even of life." Do you suppose Paul was out of the will of God in that situation? There is every indication that he was in the full will of God, doing the purpose of God, being used by God. Yet God permitted him to come into a situation of such pressure that it seemed the very life was being pressed out of him.

Have you ever felt like that? Have you ever thought, *I can't take another step. There's not one more ounce of pressure that I can endure. God, why are You permitting this?* Well, Paul and many other servants of the Lord have been through that before you, and there is a reason. God's reason is stated by Paul: "This happened that we might not rely on ourselves but on God, who raises the dead."

God wants to bring us to a place where we come to the end of all confidence in ourselves, where we have reached the absolute limit of our own knowledge, experience, strength and ability.

Once we have entered into such an experience of death, then out of that death God will bring us supernaturally into a resurrection that is on a far higher level than we were living on before we experienced that death. God is always leading us onward and upward, but if He is to bring us into a resurrection, He has to bring us through a death.

I have experienced that in my own life. I remember crying out, "God, why do You bless only the things that first die and then are resurrected?" I felt God gave me this simple answer: *Because when I'm allowed to resurrect something, I resurrect it in the form I want it to be in.*

So if you are going through an experience of death, remember there is a resurrection. Remember that God will bring you to a new revelation of Himself—a deeper, fuller knowledge of Him, if you will just hang on and trust and believe Him.

PART 5

FATHERHOOD

ONE OF THE GREAT THEMES of biblical revelation is fatherhood. Strangely enough, it is a theme that has been somewhat neglected in many Christian circles.

Fatherhood is a subject that I have not only studied in the Bible, but have also faced in my own experience. My first wife, Lydia, and I raised a family of nine. Later my second wife, Ruth, added three more children to our total family. So altogether I stand in the relationship of father to exactly one dozen persons. Most of them are grown and now have families of their own.

I have often said that there are no delinquent children, only delinquent parents! While that may be somewhat overstated, both Scripture and experience tell me that true fatherhood must be recaptured for God's purposes to be accomplished. There is so much that must happen in the lives of children that comes most naturally from a father. If, as in my case, that relationship is not warm and constant, there is much "catching up" to do later. But by God's grace we *can* become the fathers we long to be.

Let's examine this crucial subject together.

twenty

THE FATHERHOOD OF GOD

IT IS NOT WITH HUMAN FATHERHOOD that I want to begin. I want to share, first of all, about the Fatherhood of God.

There is a Father who is our God and who is also the fact behind all other facts. He created the entire universe as a Father, and He has left the imprint of His Fatherhood on every aspect of it.

In Ephesians 3:14–15 Paul prays one of his great and wonderful prayers: "I bow my knees to the Father of our Lord Jesus Christ, from whom the whole family in heaven and earth is named" (NKJV). The word that is here translated "family" is the Greek word *patria*. That word is derived directly from the Greek word for "father," so the most literal, straightforward translation would be "fatherhood."

In this connection, I would also like to give you J. B. Phillips' translation of these verses, which brings out the connection between *father* and *family* or *fatherhood*: "As I think of this great plan I fall on my knees before the Father (from whom all fatherhood, earthly or heavenly, derives its name)."

This is a remarkable fact! Fatherhood did not begin on earth; it began in heaven. Fatherhood did not begin with time or human history; it began in eternity. All fatherhood in the universe ultimately goes back to the Fatherhood of God.

Eternally God is the Father of our Lord Jesus Christ, and He is so described in many parts of the Bible. John's Gospel says, "In the beginning . . . the Word was with God" (John 1:1, NASB). That was before creation ever took place. The divine Word, the eternal Son of God, was with the Father. The Scripture says He was "in the bosom of the Father" (John 1:18, NASB). The intimate, personal relationship between the Father and the Son existed before creation ever began.

This is an absolutely distinctive feature of Christian revelation. It makes Christianity unlike any other religious faith I have ever encountered. It reveals something unique and particular about the nature of God. In God eternally there is Fatherhood. There is relationship.

When Jesus came to earth, His ultimate purpose was to bring to the Father those who would turn to Him. This is stated in many places. For example: "Christ also died for sins once for all, the just for the unjust, so that He might bring us to God" (1 Peter 3:18, NASB). Why did Jesus die? To bring us to God.

Jesus is not the end; He is the way. He said that Himself: "I am the way, and the truth, and the life; no one comes to the Father but through Me" (John 14:6, NASB). Jesus is the way but the Father is the destination.

Many times in our Christian faith we miss the purpose of God. We talk a great deal about the Lord Jesus Christ as our Savior, our Intercessor, our Mediator and so on. All this is wonderful, but it stops short of God's purpose. God's purpose is not merely that we should come to the Son, but that through the Son we should come to the Father.

There is something beautiful about the language of Jesus in His prayer in John 17. This prayer opens with the word *Father,* and that word occurs six more times in the prayer. Jesus speaks about having made known the name of God to His disciples: "I have manifested Your name to the men whom You gave Me out of the world" (verse 6, NASB). Later He says, "Holy Father, keep them in Your name, the name which You have given Me" (verse 11, NASB). And right at the end of His prayer He says again, "I have made Your name known to them, and will make it known, so that the love with which You loved Me may be in them, and I in them" (verse 26, NASB).

What name was it that Jesus came especially to make known to His disciples? It was not the sacred name *Jehovah.* The Jewish people had known that name for fifteen centuries. What was the new and special revelation, the great purpose, the name Jesus wanted the disciples to know? The name is *Father.* That is the ultimate name of God. It describes the nature of God in His eternal character more perfectly than any other word that exists in human language.

The ultimate revelation of God in the New Testament, therefore, is the revelation of God as Father. And the ultimate purpose of the New Testament, the reason Jesus Himself came, is to bring us to God. If we stop short of this revelation of God, we have stopped short of the full and final outworking of the purpose of redemption.

Provision for Three Needs

When we come into the fullness of this revelation of God and into that direct relationship with Him as Father, it supplies certain things that are conspicuously lacking in the emotional experience of perhaps the majority of the people in our culture. The three things that come out of this revelation and relationship are *identity, self-worth* and *security.*

Identity

Identity is a real problem for modern man. An interesting commentary on this need was the success of the book and TV serial *Roots*. The essence of that story was a man looking for the place from which his ancestors had come. All humanity is busy with the same search. Men and women want to know where they came from, who is behind them, how it started and who they are. Scripture and psychology agree that a person has more difficulty answering the question *Who am I?* without knowing who his or her father is.

Relationships between parents and children today have so broken down that it has produced an identity crisis. Christianity's answer to that crisis is to bring men and women into a direct, personal relationship with God the Father through Jesus Christ the Son. People who truly know God as Father no longer have an identity problem. They know who they are: They are children of God. Their Father created the universe, their Father loves them and their Father cares for them.

Self-Worth

This brings us to the second need supplied by this revelation of God the Father—our need for self-worth. I cannot count how many people I have dealt with in my ministry whose greatest problem was that they had too low a picture of themselves, which caused them many spiritual and emotional agonies. 1 John 3:1 says: "See how great a love the Father has bestowed on us, that we would be called children of God; and such we are" (NASB).

Once we comprehend that we are children of God, that God loves us intimately and personally, that He is interested in us, that He is never too busy for us and that He desires a direct and personal relationship with us, we find self-worth. I have seen this happen again and again.

Once I was going to a meeting and literally ran into a lady. We were going in opposite directions at considerable speed.

She picked herself up and said, "Mr. Prince, I've been praying that if God wanted you to speak to me, we'd meet."

"Well," I said, "we've met! But I can give you only about two minutes. I'm on my way to a meeting."

She began to tell me what her problem was, and after a while I interrupted her.

"I'm sorry," I said, "I've only got one minute left, but I think I know your problem. Will you follow me in this prayer?"

I led her in a prayer in which she thanked God because He was her Father and she was His child, that He loved her, that He cared for her, that she was special and that she belonged to the best family in the universe. Then I said, "Good-bye, I have to go."

About a month later I got a letter from the woman.

"I just want to tell you that being together with you and praying that prayer has completely changed my attitude toward life," she wrote. "For the first time I really have a sense of my own worth."

Security

The third great provision of God through the revelation of His Fatherhood is security. Behind the universe there is not just some scientific force or "big bang," but a Father who loves us.

A friend of mine was once feeling lonely and blue late at night in the deserted, windy streets of a city. He did not know if he was going to make it through. As he stood there on the street corner, he began to say, over and over again, "Father . . . Father . . . Father . . . Father . . ." As he did that, security came to him. He knew that even though things were cold and bleak around him, he was a child of God in the universe God had created for His children.

We receive each of these three things—*identity, self-worth* and *security*—when we come into the fullness of the revelation of God and into a direct relationship with Him as Father.

The Implications for Human Fatherhood

Since the eternal character and nature of God is that of Father, it follows that every father represents God. In a certain sense we may say that a good father is the most God-like thing a man can become. It is a man's highest achievement.

I remember a time when I was continually traveling from meeting to meeting and conference to conference, preaching to large crowds and finding a good response from the people. Then I heard a man make this statement: "The expert is the man away from home with a briefcase." It went to my heart like an arrow. *That really describes me,* I thought to myself. *I'm a man away from home with a briefcase. Everybody regards me as an expert. But in actual fact, what's happening in my home?*

God challenged me in an altogether new way that I had to succeed as husband and father, first and foremost, before I could succeed in any other capacity. To succeed in other capacities but fail as a father would be, in God's sight, to fail.

I believe this pattern is true of many men in our culture today. They can succeed in many capacities—on the golf course, as bank president, as author, as actor, maybe even as Christian minister—yet fail in their homes. I want to suggest to you that to fail in your home as a father is to fail, and that no other success can make up for that failure.

In 1 Corinthians 11:3 Paul speaks about a relationship between God and the home:

> I want you to understand that Christ is the head of every man [or husband], and the man is the head of a woman, and God [the Father] is the head of Christ.
>
> NASB

Since Christ is the head of the husband, and the husband, in turn, is the head of his wife and family, the husband and father represents Christ to his family. He has the same relationship to his family that Christ has to him.

There are three main ministries of Christ that are eternally associated with the Lord Jesus Christ: that of priest, that of prophet and that of king. Let me explain briefly what is involved in each ministry:

As a priest, the father represents his family to God.
As a prophet, he represents God to his family.
As a king, he governs his family on behalf of God.

twenty-one

THE FATHER AS A PRIEST

THE FATHER IS THE PRIEST of his home, representing his family to God in intercession and prayer. A father's success in the other two ministries as prophet and king are closely tied in with his success as intercessor and priest. If he succeeds as an intercessor, he will probably also succeed as a prophet and king. But if he does not understand the practice of the ministry of intercession for his family, then it will be very difficult for him to be either prophet or king in his family.

There are some beautiful examples in the Bible of fathers who practiced this ministry of intercession. At the opening of the book of Job we read that Job was a perfect and upright man before God. One day each week his seven sons and three daughters met in the house of one of his sons for feasting and fellowship. At the end of each week Job arose early, saying in his heart that maybe his sons had failed and were not right with God, so he offered sacrifices on their behalf.

The offering of these sacrifices of Job corresponds in Old Testament terminology to the ministry of intercessory prayer on

140

behalf of our children under the New Covenant in Jesus Christ. Every father is called to be an intercessor for his children.

Then we move on into the history of the nation of Israel and find them enslaved in Egypt under darkness and oppression. God made provision for their deliverance through the sacrifice of the Passover lamb. The ultimate point of separation between Israel and Egypt was the Passover, which provided for the deliverance of every Israelite family. The destroying angel came into every Egyptian home and slew the firstborn. But because of the blood of the Passover lamb, the destroying angel was not allowed to visit or destroy in any Israelite household. How was that blood applied? Who applied it?

> "Speak to all the congregation of Israel, saying: 'On the tenth day of this month every man shall take for himself a lamb, according to the house of his father, a lamb for a household.'"
> Exodus 12:3, NKJV

Who was responsible to select the lamb? The father of every family. Who was responsible to slay the lamb? The father. Who was responsible to sprinkle its blood with hyssop on the doorpost of his home? The father. In other words, the father had the God-appointed ministry of priest on behalf of his family. It was his responsibility to see that God's provision of salvation was made effective in his home. As far as I understand the revelation of Scripture, no one else could do the father's job for him. If he fulfilled his function as priest and sprinkled the blood, his family would be safe. If he failed, there was no one else who could take his place and provide protection for his family.

I believe God has caused that revelation to come to us because it is still applicable today. There is something in the spiritual realm that a father can do for his house that he cannot delegate to anybody else. He can serve with a priestly ministry for his home that God will acknowledge, but God is not obliged to acknowledge that ministry in any other person but the father. It is the father's responsibility to provide divine protection for his home.

My heart goes out to single mothers in this area. They have been placed in the role of being both parents 24 hours per day, seven days per week, with no support or respite. In such cases I would expect (and have observed) a grace poured out from God to provide identity and security to the children without a father in the home. Some of the greatest heroes today are these single moms, and they have my utmost respect and support.

In the New Testament I would like to point out a remarkable fact about the ministry of Jesus that I have learned through personal experience. People have come to me to request prayer for a child and I have learned to ask, "Are you this child's parent?" Sometimes the answer is, "No, we're just neighbors. The parents didn't want to come." God showed me that I had no scriptural basis for praying for a child like that. Jesus never ministered to a child except on the basis of the faith of one or both parents. He always required a parent to exercise faith for a child.

This is conspicuous in the story of the epileptic boy recorded in Mark 9. Jesus came down from the Mount of Transfiguration and was confronted by a scene in which His disciples had failed to cast out an epileptic spirit from a boy. Jesus asked the father how long the boy had suffered. He replied,

> "From childhood. And often he has thrown him both into the fire and into the water to destroy him. But if You can do anything, have compassion on us and help us." Jesus said to him, "If you can believe, all things are possible to him who believes."
>
> Mark 9:22–23, NKJV

One day I was gripped by the realization that Jesus held the father responsible to believe for his son. The son, because of his

142

condition, could not exercise much faith for himself, but in any case Jesus did not ask him to exercise faith. He required the father to exercise faith on his behalf. I believe it is the responsibility of parents to exercise faith in intercessory prayer on behalf of their children and to bring them to God through Jesus Christ. Search the Scriptures for yourself. You will find that Jesus never ministered to a child unless at least one parent was exercising faith on behalf of that child. He would not go contrary to such a deeply entrenched principle of God.

In Acts 16, after Paul and Silas had been imprisoned, God intervened with an earthquake, the prison doors were opened and the people's chains were loosed. Then the Philippian jailer sprang in and said,

> "Sirs, what must I do to be saved?" So they said, "Believe on the Lord Jesus Christ, and you will be saved, you and your household."
>
> Acts 16:30–31, NKJV

You will notice that the jailer, as the father of his house, was afforded the God-given privilege of exercising faith for the salvation of his whole house. Too many times, alas, in quoting that Scripture, we tend to leave out those last three words: *and your household.*

twenty-two

THE FATHER AS A PROPHET

A FATHER'S SECOND main responsibility is being the prophet for his family—that is, representing God to them.

The first thing we need to see is that inevitably a father *does* represent God to his family. He may do it well or he may do it badly but, almost inevitably, he does it. Psychiatrists, sociologists and those in ministry would almost all agree that a child normally forms his or her first impression of God from the father. I believe this was intended by God. One of the most solemn responsibilities God can give any human being is to represent Him to others.

The kind of father you had has a lot to do with your initial response and reaction to God. If you had a father who was kind, outgoing, warmhearted and easy to communicate with, you will normally find it easy to think of and to approach God in those terms. But if you had a father who was unkind, critical and always making unreasonable and excessive demands, you are liable to think of God in the same way. You will see Him as making demands that humanity can never live up to—unrealistic, legalistic and harsh. Sometimes it happens that a child has a father who is actually cruel and vicious. Frequently such a child unconsciously transfers those attributes from the natural human father to God. Consequently he or she has a negative attitude toward God based on nothing except the behavior of the father.

Two Opposite Dangers

How can a father represent God faithfully to his family—to be the prophet for good and not for evil? Paul writes the following to fathers:

> Fathers, do not provoke your children to anger, but bring them up in the discipline and instruction of the Lord.
>
> Ephesians 6:4, NASB

> Fathers, do not exasperate your children, so that they will not lose heart.
>
> Colossians 3:21, NASB

The New Testament, like the Old Testament, places the responsibility for the spiritual education and instruction of the children fairly and squarely on the shoulders of the father. Obviously mothers have great influence over their children and a lot to contribute to their spiritual development, but primarily it is the father who is responsible for providing spiritual instruction. If he does not do it, there is no one else who can exactly take over that responsibility.

But again we must remember and speak to single moms. If you, for whatever reason, have been placed in the situation of being both mom and dad, expect God's intervention and ability to persevere. Trust your parental instincts and guidance, for God will bring your children safely through by your wisdom and instruction. For years in Israel, before I arrived on the scene, my first wife, Lydia, was the parent to our eight adopted daughters (and many others for short seasons). I am sure our daughters can testify to Lydia's incredible impact as a single mom.

The majority of American fathers, if they are aware that they have any responsibility for the instruction of their children, are quite content to transfer it to the Sunday school, to the church, to the pastor or to the youth leader. Very often such a parent, if his child is in a church or youth group and then goes astray, will blame the church or youth group. But the father can never divest himself of the primary responsibility for raising his children in the discipline and instruction of the Lord. It is one of his sacred responsibilities, which is not transferable.

Paul indicates that, in doing this, a father must guard against two opposite dangers. The first danger is *rebelliousness* in the child. The father guards against rebellion by maintaining firm discipline—not allowing his children to become wayward or irresponsible, not allowing them to answer back, and expecting them to do what they are told promptly, quietly, obediently. It is much easier to give instruction to children who are brought up that way.

But a father must also guard against the opposite extreme, which is *discouragement*. If a father is unduly severe, critical and demanding, the child may become discouraged and take the attitude, "Well, it's no good. Nothing I do ever pleases him, so I might as well not bother to try." The warnings Paul gives are twofold: "Don't provoke them. Don't exasperate them."

I have dealt with many people with severe emotional problems who came to me for help. I cannot tell you how many times I discovered that their negative attitudes—lack of self-worth, feeling of failure, frustration—went back to a time when, as children, they experienced negative treatment such as criticism, being put down or scolded unfairly in front of others. That treatment left marks or wounds in their souls that had not healed for maybe twenty or thirty years. Fathers must be careful to maintain discipline, on the one hand, but

146

not to discourage or exasperate their children, on the other hand, by unfair or excessive demands.

Let Them Talk to You

In order to meet his responsibilities to his family, a father must always keep in mind the need for regular, ongoing communication with his children. If he does not maintain that kind of communication, he cannot fulfill his responsibilities. The communication between a father and his child is usually most effective in a non-religious setting. If children associate the instruction their father gives them with something stiff, formal and religious, they tend, in the end, to resent both the religion and the instruction. I can think of a good many cases of people whose problems originated in that kind of setting.

It is essential in communicating with children not merely to talk to them but to let them talk to you. Most people who deal with wayward or delinquent children agree that they nearly always have one common complaint: "Our parents never listen to us." So cultivate the practice of listening. Let your child talk. Let him express himself. Let her come out with her problem, and do not try to do it in too religious an atmosphere.

This principle is stated in the law, in which Moses gave the Israelites clear and practical instructions on how to bring up their children:

> "You shall lay up these my words of mine in your heart and in your soul. . . . You shall teach them to your children, speaking of them when you sit in your house, when you walk by the way, when you lie down, and when you rise up. And you shall write them on the doorposts of your house and on your gates, that your days and the days of your children may be multiplied in the land of which the LORD swore to your fathers to give them, like the days of the heavens above the earth."
>
> Deuteronomy 11:18–21, NKJV

Heaven on Earth

I was impressed when I discovered that the phrase *heaven on earth* came from the Bible. Furthermore it is a description of what God expects the families of His people to be like. But I looked around at our modern civilization and said to myself, *How many families in this nation today could be described as "heaven on earth"?* I would say, frankly, it is a very small proportion.

One main reason for this is that fathers have failed to do what Moses said they should do. Moses said, in effect, "Teach the Word of God—the truths of your faith—to your children. Speak about them when you sit down, when you rise up and when you walk by the way." In other words, let the Word of God be a central theme in your family's life. Do not simply reserve the teaching of Scripture for church, Sunday school or youth group. Let God's Word have a natural place in your daily life and in your communication with your family. Let it be natural and practical. Let your children see how it works out in real-life situations.

I would like to quote the testimony of the late Dr. V. Raymond Edman, one-time president of Wheaton College, who said: "Looking back on the way I brought up my children, if I had to do it over, I'd spend more time with them in simple, non-religious activities." To that I would have to say, "Amen." If I could live some of the time I have spent with my children again, that is what I would do, too. Dr. Edman found that the things his grown children remembered most were the informal times of just being together.

Real communication with a child is not achieved in five minutes. Often the most important things are said with a child in a casual or offhand way at a time you least expect it—gardening, mowing the lawn, fishing, cleaning out the garage, finding out why the car will not run. It is situations like these that lend themselves to real communication between parents and children. It is in these kinds of situations that a father should be able to transmit to his child the deep principles of the Word of God. Just having "a family altar" will not by itself necessarily do it. A lot depends on how you spend the rest of your time.

twenty-three

THE FATHER AS A KING

THE FUNCTION OF A KING is to rule or govern, and this is the third ministry of the father in his home. But in modern America the word *king* is not always acceptable, although the word is used throughout the Bible. If you do not like the word *king,* we can substitute the word *governor.* In any case, the function of the father is to rule or govern his household on behalf of God.

In 1 Timothy, Paul discusses the qualifications for a man who wants to hold the position of elder, overseer or bishop. Regardless of the word used, Paul is describing a man who is to lead or govern God's people. The most important of all the qualifications for that office is the condition of the man's home. How does he function there? This is what Paul says:

> He must have proper authority in his own household, and be able to control and command the respect of his children. (For if a man cannot rule in his own house how can he look after a church of God?)
>
> 1 Timothy 3:4–5, Phillips

150

A man is expected to rule in his own house. He is expected to exercise authority and to have children who are respectful, obedient and under his control. If a man cannot achieve that at home, Paul says, he has no hope of succeeding as a ruler, governor or leader in God's church.

The word used for "rule" means, in Greek, "to stand out in front" or "to stand at the head of." It contains various related ideas. Here are a few different ways you can understand it: to rule, to lead, to stand at the head, to protect, to control. Essentially it means that the father is the head of his home. He is out in front. He sets an example. He stands between his family and all the dangers and pressures of life. He is a man. He has what it takes. He has what modern speech calls "guts." It takes guts to be a man and to be a father!

The Three Corresponding Elements

Paul goes on to say that successful leadership at home is essential for leadership in the church. There is a strong reason for this: The home is really the church in miniature, in microcosm or in embryo.

In a church there are three main elements: the pastor or shepherd; the deacon or helper; and the congregation or flock. These correspond to the three main elements in the home. There the father has the responsibilities of the pastor or shepherd. The wife, according to Scripture, is the helper, created (like the deacon) to help her husband. The children are the congregation or flock. All the basics that make up a proper New Testament church, God has built into the family. He says, in effect, to the father of the family, "You make it succeed in your little church, the one I've committed to you in your own home, and then you'll qualify for promotion in the church of God."

Let me add, as a matter of observation and experience, that you can build a large congregation of people who attend a church, but in the last resort, a congregation is no stronger than the families that make it up. If the families are not in order, the church cannot be in order.

Why Abraham?

Abraham is a picture of a father who accepted and fulfilled his responsibility to rule, govern or be king of his home. Have you ever wondered why God chose Abraham? Doubtless there were hundreds of thousands of his contemporaries all over the earth's surface. Of those hundreds of thousands, God chose him. Is it an unrevealed mystery why God chose this man to be the head of a new race on which the salvation of all other races would depend? No, it is not. In a significant passage the Lord reveals why He chose Abraham to be the head of the new nation that was ultimately to bring redemption to all humanity:

> The LORD said, "Shall I hide from Abraham what I am doing, since Abraham shall surely become a great and mighty nation, and all the nations of the earth shall be blessed in him? For I have known him, in order that he may command his children and his household after him, that they keep the way of the LORD, to do righteousness and justice, that the LORD may bring to Abraham what He has spoken to him."
>
> Genesis 18:17–19, NKJV

He Was a Father

Look first at the meaning of Abraham's name. Originally his name was Abram, which means "exalted father." When God made His covenant, blessed Abram and promised him a great number of descendants, God changed his name to Abraham, which means "father of a multitude." You will see in both forms that the first fact about this man's name is that he was a father. That is tremendously significant. God chose Abraham as a father.

He Fulfilled His Obligations

Second, when the duties of fatherhood are carried out, it builds a mighty nation. God said of Abraham that he "shall surely become a great and mighty nation." Why? Because he could be relied on to fulfill his obligations as a father.

He Governed His Family

Third, God Himself states why He chose Abraham: "I have known him, in order that he may command his children and his household after him, that they keep the way of the LORD, to do righteousness and justice, that the LORD may bring to Abraham what He has spoken to him." What did God see in Abraham that made Him choose him? He saw that this man would command his children and his household after him to keep the way of the Lord. God could rely on Abraham to fulfill his duties as governor of his family.

That word *command* is a strong word, almost a military word. Some mothers or wives may be asking, "Are you speaking about being a dictator?" No, but I am speaking about a man who is a man—a man who knows his position and responsibility. There are some situations in which a man under God is responsible to command his household. He is responsible to say, "In order to please God and have His blessing, this is the way we're going to do it in our home. We're *not* going to do this, but we *are* going to do that."

A father has the right, I believe, to determine some of the basic rules of the household: what time they will eat together, what time the younger children must come in, the kind of entertainment the children are permitted, the amount of time they spend in front of the television and the kinds of programs they watch. It is not merely the father's privilege to command his family in these respects; it is his duty. He should not make decisions such as these without consulting his wife and making sure she is in agreement. Nevertheless the final responsibility for order in the house rests with him. He is the one who must answer to God for his family.

God said, "I'll bring on Abraham that which I've promised because I can trust him to do that for Me."

He Walked in Faith

Fourth, throughout the rest of the Scripture, Abraham is set forth as a pattern for all subsequent believers. In fact, the New Testament says we are the children of Abraham by faith and that we are to walk in the steps of the faith of our father, Abraham. Walking in the steps of Abraham's faith means that we behave in our homes as Abraham behaved in his home.

Let me draw a contrast. There was another man who walked a long way with Abraham, who knew a lot of what Abraham knew and who saw a lot of what God did for Abraham. His name was Lot. When the time came for Abraham and Lot to separate because their flocks and herds were too numerous for them to stay together, Abraham, gentleman that he was, said to Lot, "You choose. Whichever way you go, I'll go the opposite." Lot chose to go toward Sodom, a place of extreme sinfulness. The next time we read about Lot, he and his family were inside Sodom and the judgment of God was about to fall on the city. Lot tried desperately to get his sons-in-law and most of his family out, and failed. As he himself escaped and looked back on the smoldering ruins of Sodom, he must have realized that many of his family had been destroyed in it and that he was responsible for taking them there in the first place.

What a fearful responsibility rested on the shoulders of Lot as a father! He led his children into a place of sin and ultimate judgment and could not get them out again.

Fathers, you may lead your children into Sodom, but you may not be able to lead them out again. Walk the way Abraham walked. In no area is this more important than in your family.

twenty-four

WHEN FATHERS FAIL

SUPPOSE A FATHER FAILS. What happens to his family? Or suppose the fathers in a nation fail. What happens to that nation? Because God knew that Abraham would fulfill his duties as a father, God promised that he would become a great and mighty nation. But what about a nation whose fathers do not fulfill their duties?

In Deuteronomy 28 Moses lists two results—first, the blessings that will come on God's people if they obey Him; and second, the curses that will come on them if they disobey Him. The first fourteen verses contain the blessings. The remaining 54 verses, 15 through 68, list the curses for the disobedience of not walking in God's way and not keeping God's law. There are many remarkable curses listed; I want to point out just one:

> You shall beget sons and daughters, but they shall not be yours; for they shall go into captivity.
>
> Deuteronomy 28:41, NKJV

The language Moses uses for *you* is masculine. In other words, this passage is addressed primarily to fathers. Also, the word *beget* refers mainly to the father's part in procreating children. So this is addressed chiefly (but not exclusively) to fathers. It says, "You will have sons and daughters but you will not enjoy them."

It came to me with a shock one day that not enjoying our children is a curse! I began to ask myself, *How many American parents today really enjoy their children?* I was reminded of a pastor friend of mine with a large family of children who I heard pray one day, "Lord, help us to remember that children are a blessing and not a burden." I did not feel somehow that he was praying with very strong faith.

The majority of American parents, I think, do not really enjoy their children. What is the reason? It is a curse for disobedience. God provides children as the greatest blessing He can give to men and women. When fathers and mothers, and especially fathers, do not walk in the way of the Lord, then that blessing is no longer a blessing. Moses warned the fathers of Israel that if they did not keep God's way and walk in it, then "you will not enjoy your children, for they shall go into captivity."

In the last few decades we have seen millions of American children go into various kinds of satanic captivity—drugs, illicit sex, addiction to the Internet, cults, self-mutilation (body-piercing and tattoos), subculture groups like Goths.

This is captivity just as surely as if an invading army had come into the country and carried them off as prisoners. Why have these millions of American children gone into captivity? The answer is here in Deuteronomy: because their fathers failed in their duties. The primary responsibility for that state of affairs in modern America rests at the door of American fathers.

We hear a lot about juvenile delinquents. There are hardly any juvenile delinquents until there are first adult delinquents. It takes adult delinquents to bring forth juvenile delinquents.

I pointed out in chapter 21 that one of the father's responsibilities to his family is that of a priest. In Malachi the Lord states what is required of a priest:

156

The lips of a priest should keep knowledge, and people should seek the law from his mouth; for he is the messenger of the LORD of hosts.

Malachi 2:7, NKJV

It is the responsibility of the priest to know the law of the Lord and to interpret it to the Lord's people. So the priest is the messenger—or perhaps a better word would be *representative*—of the Lord to His people. This applies (as we have already seen) to the father as priest. His lips should keep knowledge. His children and family should seek the Lord God at his mouth. He should be God's representative to them.

What happens if priests fail in this function? In Hosea God declares what He will do to a family, to a nation or to a civilization:

My people are destroyed for lack of knowledge. Because you have rejected knowledge, I also will reject you from being priest for Me; because you have forgotten the law of your God, I also will forget your children.

Hosea 4:6, NKJV

That is a powerful word to fathers. God says, in effect, "I expected you to be the priest of your family. But because you have rejected the knowledge that your family needs"—and this refers not to scientific knowledge, but the knowledge of the way and the Word of the Lord—"I am going to reject you. I will no longer accept you as priest. And when your priestly ministry on behalf of your children is no longer accepted by Me," God says, "then I will also forget your children."

That is frightening! To think that God would say to us, as parents, "You have so failed in your responsibility that I am going to forget your children. I am going to be toward them as if they were not there. I am going to write them off. They are of no more consequence or significance before Me." This civilization of ours is filled with God-forgotten children. Why? Because their fathers did not keep the law of the Lord.

Let me say it this way: The father who rejects the knowledge of God's law loses his right to be priest to his family. And when his priestly ministry is no longer available, God says, "I will forget your children."

In closing this section, I want to turn to the last two verses of Malachi. Have you ever reflected on the fact that the last word of the Old Testament in most translations is the word *curse?* It is a solemn thought that if God had no more to say to mankind after the Old Testament, His last word to humanity would have been a curse. Thank God for the New Testament that shows the way out of the curse!

Here is what God says:

"Behold, I will send you Elijah the prophet before the coming of the great and dreadful day of the LORD. And he will turn the hearts of the fathers to the children, and the hearts of the children to their fathers, lest I come and strike the earth with a curse."

Malachi 4:5–6, NKJV

I am impressed by the tremendous insight of prophetic revelation in that, well over two thousand years ago, Malachi was able to foresee the greatest and most urgent social problem of our day. What is that problem? Divided, strife-torn homes. Fathers and children out of relationship. The children rebellious, the fathers negligent. The prophet warns us that if this state of affairs does not change, it will bring a curse on that family, nation or civilization. God's Word faces us with just two alternatives in our current situation: We may either restore family relationships and survive, or we may allow family relationships to deteriorate and go the way they have been going the last decades. If we do the latter, we will perish under God's curse. Those are the alternatives.

In a very significant sense, our destiny will be settled by the fathers. It is the fathers God holds responsible. Because God could trust Abraham to be the kind of father He wanted, He said, "He will become a great and mighty nation." But the contrary is also true: Where fathers fail and do not fulfill their responsibilities, a nation can no longer remain great. I believe that is the very crisis that confronts our nation today. Will the fathers return to God and face their responsibilities to their families in the sight of God? Or will the present moral and social breakdown, which originated in the family and is destroying the family, continue and come to its ultimate consequence, which is a curse?

God requires the fathers to turn to the children. Then He promises the children will return to their fathers. It is the decision of the fathers that determines the destiny of the nation.

PART 6

FROM CURSE
TO BLESSING

SOME YEARS AGO I found myself confronted with a number of situations that did not yield to the normal forms of spiritual warfare with which I was familiar. I became aware of this through dealing with several people whose problems could actually be traced to previous generations. I found in my study that blessing and cursing is a major theme in Scripture, with one or the other mentioned some nine hundred times! I wondered how I could have missed this important theme.

I found myself rather alone as I delved into this area of blessing and cursing, although now I have been joined in this understanding by many fine Bible teachers and ministers. I urge you to open yourself completely to the examination of the Holy Spirit as to whether there has been the shadow of a curse over your life and family. And, as always, may I remind you that the remedy for every problem is found in the cross of Jesus! The cross is the key to the storehouse of all God's provisions.

May the Holy Spirit fully reveal to you that Christ was made a curse that you may inherit the blessing.

twenty-five

CHRIST WAS MADE A CURSE

IF YOU HAVE ANY NEED or problem whatsoever in your life, there is one place, and only one place, to which you must go to find God's provision or solution—the cross of Jesus. Through what Jesus accomplished by His death on the cross, every provision of God—spiritual, physical and material, for time and eternity—has been made available for you. There is no other basis than the cross for all the provisions of God. Only through the cross can you come to God and receive His provisions and blessings.

In order to do that, you need to remember the basic nature of what happened when Jesus died on the cross. At that point, as you recall from Part 2, an exchange took place, divinely ordained by God and predicted many centuries before by the prophets of Israel. It is all summed up in one key verse. (Scripture is quoted from the NKJV here and throughout this section, except where marked.)

All we like sheep have gone astray; we have turned, every one,
to his own way; and the LORD has laid on Him the iniquity
of us all.

Isaiah 53:6

This is the absolute center of everything God has to offer
us. It is entirely the grace of God. We have no claim on God,
nor could we have demanded this from Him. In His infinite
grace and mercy, God Himself ordained this exchange.

Let me restate it very briefly: God laid on Jesus the iniquity of us all. We saw in chapter 6 that *iniquity* includes our
rebellion and all the evil consequences of rebellion. These consequences, which by justice should have come on us, came
upon Jesus on the cross by divine appointment. This is the
negative side of the exchange.

The positive side is that, in return, all the good that was
due to the sinless obedience of Jesus is available to us.

More simply, God visited on Jesus the evil due to us that in
return God could make available the good due to Jesus. Or,
the evil came on Jesus that the good might be made available
to us. From whatever aspect you view the cross, you see the
truth of a divinely ordained exchange. It was initiated solely
out of God's grace and mercy. Thank God, His grace and mercy
have ordained this exchange and made this provision.

Recall from our summary in chapter 8 a few of the aspects
of this exchange, in very simple terms:

Jesus was punished that we might be forgiven.

Jesus was physically wounded that we might be physically
healed.

Jesus was made sin that we might be made righteousness.

Jesus tasted our death that we might share His eternal life.

Jesus endured our poverty that we might share His
abundance.

Jesus bore our shame that we might share His glory.

164

Jesus was rejected by God the Father that we might have acceptance.

Let us focus on another aspect, the one to which the Holy Spirit sovereignly directed me some years ago. I have never found it referred to in any book I have read or any sermon I have heard. Yet if we can understand and apply the truth contained in it, it has the potential to revolutionize the whole course of our lives. I have witnessed the impact that this truth produces both on individuals and on communities. This aspect of the exchange is described in Galatians:

Christ has redeemed us from the curse of the law, having become a curse for us (for it is written, "Cursed is everyone who hangs on a tree"), that the blessing of Abraham might come upon the Gentiles in Christ Jesus. . . .

Galatians 3:13–14

The exchange there between the evil and the good is obvious. The evil is the curse; the good is the blessing. Jesus was actually made a curse when He hung on the cross. The words of God through Moses, "Cursed is everyone who hangs on a tree," are according to Deuteronomy 21:23, the cross being a tree. Christ was made a curse on the cross that we might qualify for and receive the blessing.

In order to receive this provision, it is necessary to understand the nature of both blessings and curses. If you do not, you will not be able to avail yourself of this provision.

Both blessings and curses are major themes of Scripture. The words *bless* and *blessing* occur in the Bible about 430 times. The word *curse,* in various forms, occurs about 160 times. In other words, the Bible has a great deal to say about both. Both are absolutely real; we must understand this. They are so real that Jesus had to be made a curse that we might be redeemed from the curse and receive the blessing.

Some people are inclined to think that blessings are real but not curses. That is illogical. For any pair of opposites we care to think of, if one is real, the other *must* be real: day and night, heat and cold, good and evil, and strong and weak. We cannot simply focus on one and ignore the other. So it is with blessings and curses. Blessings are real and curses are also real.

I have traveled widely and ministered to congregations of many different backgrounds, denominations and nationalities. Everywhere I go, most of God's people do not know how to discern blessings and curses. I have often asked people as I preach, "Tell me, are you enjoying the blessings or are you enduring the curses?" There are many Christians who should be enjoying blessings but who are actually enduring curses. There are two reasons for this: first, they do not know how to recognize what is a blessing and what is a curse; and second, if they are under a curse, they do not understand the basis on which they can be released.

In the chapters in this section, I will explain the nature of both blessings and curses; how they operate; how to recognize if a curse is at work in your life from which you need deliverance; and how to pass from curse to blessing, with the process and prayer of release. The Bible has much to teach us about all these areas. If we remain ignorant, it will be at our own cost. We will miss much of the total provision God has made for us through the sacrificial death of Jesus on the cross.

twenty-six

NATURE OF BLESSINGS AND CURSES

WHEN JESUS HUNG on the cross, every Jew who knew his Scriptures knew that Christ had been made a curse. What they did not understand, and what can be revealed only by the Holy Spirit, is the reason He was made a curse. Jesus was made a curse that, in return, we might be redeemed from the curse and inherit the blessing of God.

Blessings and curses essentially take the form of *words*. They may be spoken, written or merely uttered inwardly. These are not just ordinary words but vessels of supernatural power. Blessings produce good effects and curses produce evil effects. Blessings proceed from God or people representing God. Satan cannot bless anybody but he can curse. Curses proceed from Satan, therefore, or people representing him.

An important point to remember is this: *Once released, both blessings and curses tend to continue on through time until they are revoked.* Normally, once a curse or blessing has been released, it will continue until something happens to cancel or revoke it. This means there can be forces at work in our

lives that were originally set in motion in previous generations. Consequently we may be dealing with things in our
lives—circumstances, families, even temperament—that cannot be explained solely in terms of what has happened in our
lifetime or personal experience. The root cause for them may
go back a long way, even hundreds or thousands of years.

Biblical Examples

History contains many examples of the outworking of both
blessings and curses. I will begin by taking an example of a
blessing from Genesis:

> The Angel of the LORD called to Abraham a second time out
> of heaven, and said: "By Myself I have sworn, says the LORD,
> because you have done this thing, and have not withheld your
> son, your only son, in blessing I will bless you, and in multi-
> plying I will multiply your descendants as the stars of the
> heaven and as the sand which is on the seashore; and your
> descendants shall possess the gate of their enemies. In your
> seed [or *descendants*] all the nations of the earth shall be
> blessed, because you have obeyed My voice."
>
> Genesis 22:15–18

God spoke at the point at which Abraham was willing to actually offer his son Isaac as a sacrifice on Mount Moriah. This blessing was pronounced four thousand years ago and is still at work
in history today! One evidence is this book you are reading. The
blessing that comes to you through it comes through Jesus Christ,
the seed of Abraham. Because of that blessing pronounced four
thousand years ago, you are being blessed right now by receiving the message of this book. So, you see, blessings continue
from generation to generation, from century to century.

Let's look at some examples of curses. First, a curse pronounced by God Himself when He called Abraham to leave Ur

of the Chaldees and go to another land. Some of the promises
God gave Abraham were these:

> "I will bless those who bless you, and I will curse him who curses
> you; and in you all the families of the earth shall be blessed."
>
> Genesis 12:3

Notice that in the middle of the blessings there is a curse:
"I will curse him who curses you."

The same was stated later on when Isaac, the son of Abraham, blessed his son Jacob:

> "Let peoples serve you, and nations bow down to you. Be
> master over your brethren, and let your mother's sons bow
> down to you. Cursed be everyone who curses you, and blessed
> be those who bless you!"
>
> Genesis 27:29

In essence, Isaac said, "If anybody curses Jacob, God will
curse him." This is something that continues in history. In
simple, modern-day language, it is God's protection against
anti-Semitism—the attitude and spirit that curses Abraham,
Isaac, Jacob and their descendants, the Jewish people. Anybody who yields to the spirit of anti-Semitism or makes negative utterances and false statements against the Jewish people
is exposing himself or herself to that curse pronounced by
God almost four thousand years ago.

If you look at the history of all the nations and empires in
the last four thousand years that have persecuted the Jewish
people and sought to destroy them, you will find that every
one of them has come under the curse of God. This is a fact
of history. The curse is still at work in our world today. We have
only to consider the events of the 1930s and 1940s in Germany
and Europe to see how true this is today.

Another remarkable example of a biblical curse still in effect
is found in David's beautiful poetic lament when Saul and

Jonathan, Saul's son and David's beloved friend, were killed in battle against the Philistines. Since they died on the mountains of Gilboa, David addressed those mountains directly:

> O mountains of Gilboa,
> Let there be no dew
>   nor let there be rain upon you,
> Nor fields of offerings.
> For the shield of the mighty
>   is cast away there!
> The shield of Saul,
>   not anointed with oil.
>
> 2 Samuel 1:21

The Jewish people, as you may know, have been remarkably successful in reforestation. They have planted trees on every kind of hill and mountain. But they cannot succeed in making them grow in Mount Gilboa. Why? Because when David said to that particular group of hills approximately three thousand years ago, "Let there be no dew nor let there be rain," he was uttering a curse—one that is still in effect.

Can you see how real this is? Many of us need to adjust our thinking; we are grappling with unseen forces that we do not understand.

Let's look at an example of a curse pronounced by a man representing God. The man is Joshua, and the curse was pronounced after the destruction by Israel of the city of Jericho:

> Joshua charged them at that time, saying, "Cursed be the man before the LORD who rises up and builds this city Jericho; he shall lay its foundation with his firstborn, and with his youngest he shall set up its gates."
>
> Joshua 6:26

Approximately five hundred years later in the history of Israel, a certain man named Hiel of Bethel did the very thing against which Joshua had pronounced a curse. This is what 1 Kings says about him:

> In [the days of Ahab] Hiel the Bethelite built Jericho; he laid its foundations with the loss of Abiram his firstborn, and set up its gates with the loss of his youngest son Segub, according to the word of the LORD, which He spoke by Joshua the son of Nun.
>
> 1 Kings 16:34, NASB

Hiel did what Joshua had put a curse upon, and it cost him the lives of his two sons. Words that had been spoken five hundred years earlier resulted in the deaths of those two young men. Can you picture the doctors of the day analyzing their deaths? What would they discover? Would they understand that it was due to words spoken by a servant of God five hundred years before? Can you see that we wrestle with things in our lifetime the cause of which may go back centuries?

The last biblical example I want to consider is Jesus and the fig tree. He approached the tree looking for figs to eat and found none because it was not the season for figs. So He said, "Let no one eat fruit from you ever again" (Mark 11:14). That's all Jesus said; He just spoke to the tree. Some people would consider it crazy to speak to a tree. The tree, however, felt the impact of what Jesus said.

> In the morning, as [the disciples] passed by, they saw the fig tree dried up from the roots. And Peter, remembering, said to Him, "Rabbi, look! The fig tree which you cursed has withered away."
>
> verses 20–21

This is powerful! Jesus did not lay His hand on the fig tree or take an axe to it, but in the Spirit of God spoke words charged with supernatural power. Within 24 hours those words caused the fig tree to wither. That is the power of both curses and blessings. They are words charged with supernatural power and the source of many things that happen in our lives.

Historical Examples

Let's look at two examples from later history. Both of them go back to the 1600s and take place in the land of Scotland. Each of these was told to me personally by the persons involved, both of them born-again Christians.

The first is from a woman I met in Australia in December 1984. When she had heard my teaching on curses, she spoke to me and later sent me a letter in which she showed me a written curse that had been pronounced on her clan back in Scotland by the Archbishop of Edinburgh. It is a most blood-curdling curse! She told me, in effect, "Our family today is still struggling against the effects of this curse."

The second example is from November 1985. In Scotland I met a descendant of an aristocratic Scottish family in Aberdeenshire. He, too, recognized that he and his family were under a curse. In the 1600s there had been a war between two Scottish clans, his clan and another. The members of his clan had murdered the members of the other clan, including a pregnant woman. As she died, that pregnant woman pronounced a curse on his clan. He told me (and he was a very sober, intelligent man!), "That curse is still at work."

In both cases these believers felt the effects of the curses—unnatural accidents, sicknesses, family disputes, financial problems, continuing frustrations. That is how real both blessings and curses are.

172

twenty-seven

HOW TO RECOGNIZE A CURSE

PAUL LAYS GREAT EMPHASIS on the word *curse*. In Galatians 3:13 it occurs three times: "Christ has redeemed us from the *curse* of the law, having become a *curse* for us (for it is written, '*Cursed* is everyone who hangs on a tree')" (emphasis added). Then he adds, "That the blessing of Abraham might come upon the Gentiles in Christ Jesus" (verse 14). Most Christians, however, do not understand this particular provision made by God and have not, therefore, availed themselves of it.

As I stated previously, blessings and curses are words charged with supernatural power for good or evil and, once released, they generally continue from generation to generation until they are revoked or canceled.

Let me tell you a little incident that awakened me to this. I had been teaching in a church and had come to the end of my preaching. As I stood behind the pulpit wondering what to do next, I saw a family—father, mother and teenaged

173

daughter—in the front row on my left. God seemed to say to me, *There is a curse over that family.*

So I walked up to the father and said, "Sir, God has shown me that there is a curse over your family. Would you like me to release you from it in the name of Jesus?"

"Yes," he said immediately.

I stepped back behind the pulpit, said a short prayer, saw a visible physical reaction in each one as I released them from the curse.

Then I noticed that the girl, about eighteen years old, had her left leg in a cast from the thigh down to the bottom of her foot. So I stepped back and said to the father, "Would you like me to pray for your daughter's leg?"

"Yes," he said, "but you need to know she has broken the same leg three times in eighteen months and that doctors say it will not heal."

If I heard that today, I would know immediately that there was a curse. It is unnatural to break the same leg three times in eighteen months.

In any case, I prayed for her leg, and the next time she went back to the hospital, as I learned later, the leg was healed.

As I meditated on it, I realized that God had shown me there was a curse in that family, because if the curse had not been revoked, the leg would not have been healed. The curse was the barrier to the healing of the daughter's leg. A curse is often a barrier to people's receiving healing.

Guidelines for Recognizing Curses

There are certain guidelines that will help you to recognize if there is a curse at work in your life.

If there is a curse operating in your life, it is very probable that you have been struggling against something that you were never really able to master or overcome. The thing you are struggling against is a curse. If you look only in your own lifetime, you may not find the cause of it. In light of this, let me first give you a general picture of what a curse is like. I will use the best descriptive language I can and trust that the Holy Spirit will quicken to you whatever you particularly need in order to understand.

A curse is something like a dark shadow or an evil hand from the past—oppressing you, pressing you down, holding you back, tripping you up and propelling you in a direction you do not really wish to take. It is like a negative atmosphere that surrounds you, which seems to be stronger at some times than others, but from which you are never totally free.

If I were to choose one key word, it would be the word *frustration*. You reach a certain level of achievement or progress in your life, for example, and you seem to have all the needed qualifications for success, yet something goes wrong. You start over, you reach the same level, then something goes wrong again. This seems to be the pattern of your life, yet there is no obvious reason for it.

I cannot tell you how many people I have dealt with who have told me a life story with many different details, but the pattern is still there. Often they will say something like, "The same thing used to happen in my father's life," or, "I remember my grandfather telling me about this." Somehow they are vaguely aware that this thing did not begin in their own lifetime.

This pattern may occur in various areas—business, personal relationships (especially marriage and family), career, finances, health. In all probability, whatever area it may be, that dark shadow or evil hand is a curse over your life, perhaps going back many generations.

Forms of Blessings and Curses

Let me give you some specific forms that curses may take. Anybody who has a problem in this area should take time to study, meditate on and pray over Deuteronomy 28. I will offer a very brief summation of the blessings and the curses. First the blessings:

Exaltation (being lifted up)
Health
Reproductiveness in every area
Prosperity
Victory
God's favor

The curses, essentially, are the opposite:

Humiliation
Failure to reproduce (barrenness in almost any area is nearly
    always the outworking of a curse)
Mental and physical sickness
Family breakdown
Poverty
Defeat
Oppression
Failure
God's disfavor

Moses said to Israel, "If God's blessing is on your life, you will be the head and not the tail; you will be above and not beneath" (see Deuteronomy 28:13). That is the difference between blessing and curse. I have often asked people, "Are you living like a head or a tail? Are you taking the initiative, making the decisions? Or are you just being dragged around like a tail by forces you have no control over? Are you living above or are you living under?"

I once heard about one Christian who said to another, "How are you doing?" The other one answered, "Well, under the circumstances, I'm not doing too badly." The first one replied,

"Well, what are you doing *under* the circumstances?" You should not be *under* the circumstances. If the blessing of God is in your life, you will be above the circumstances, not under them.

Both blessings and curses are not limited normally to a single individual. They apply more often to a family, community or nation, and sometimes to a whole civilization.

Common Indicators

I have made my own list of seven common indications of curses that I have found in people's lives. This was done purely on the basis of experience and observation.

1. Mental and/or emotional breakdown.
2. Repeated or chronic sicknesses, especially if these are hereditary or without clear medical diagnosis.
3. Repeated miscarriages or related female problems.
4. The breakdown of marriage and family alienation, where a family falls apart.
5. Continuing financial insufficiency, especially where the income appears to be sufficient. A little with God's blessing does more than a lot with a curse on it.
6. Being accident-prone.
7. In a family, a history of suicides or unnatural deaths.

Now let's look at the kinds of things that cause either blessings or curses in a person's life.

twenty-eight

WHAT CAUSES BLESSINGS OR CURSES?

IT IS IMPORTANT to understand that there is always a cause for both blessings and curses. In connection with curses, this is what Solomon says:

> Like a flitting sparrow,
>   like a flying swallow,
> So a curse without cause shall not alight.
> Proverbs 26:2

Whenever a curse alights, in other words, there is a cause behind it. It is often important to discover the cause and to distinguish between primary and secondary causes. In each case the primary cause of both blessings and curses is simple.

Primary Causes

Let's look, first of all, at blessings. Moses states the primary cause for God's blessing in Deuteronomy 28:

It shall come to pass, if you diligently obey the voice of the
LORD your God, to observe carefully all His commandments
which I command you today, that the LORD your God will
set you high above all nations of the earth. And all these blessings shall come upon you and overtake you, because you obey
the voice of the LORD your God.

Deuteronomy 28:1–2

The causes of all blessing are *listening to God's voice* and
doing what He says. This is clearly exemplified in the case of
Abraham when he offered up his son Isaac. Recall what God
said to him:

"In blessing I will bless you, and in multiplying I will multiply
your descendants as the stars of the heaven and as the sand
which is on the seashore; and your descendants shall possess
the gate of their enemies. In your seed all the nations of the
earth shall be blessed, because you have obeyed My voice."

Genesis 22:17–18

The cause for Abraham's blessing was that he heard and
obeyed the voice of God.

The basic cause for curses is stated in Deuteronomy 28:15:

"It shall come to pass, if you do not obey the voice of the
LORD your God, to observe carefully all His commandments
and His statutes which I command you today, that all these
curses will come upon you and overtake you."

The root cause of all curses, therefore, is *not* hearing and
obeying God's voice.

Notice that both curses and blessings "overtake" us. We do
not really have to pursue them; we just have to fulfill the
conditions, either positive or negative. If we fulfill the positive
conditions, then blessings overtake us. If we fulfill the negative conditions, then curses overtake us. It does not matter
how hard we try; we cannot go so fast that they will not overtake us!

Secondary Causes

From these primary roots spring many different kinds of behavior that I call "secondary causes." A list of twelve secondary causes of curses that proceed from God is given in Deuteronomy 27:15–26. God warns Israel, "If you do these things, you'll come under a curse." These twelve secondary causes can be summed up as follows (with the first four being the main causes).

1. Idolatry, False Gods and the Occult

We need to remember that involvement with the occult is the same as worshiping false gods. It means going to false gods, or the servants of false gods, for help that we should seek only from the true God.

I want to emphasize particularly the consequences of idolatry or the occult as stated by God:

> "You shall have no other gods before [or *beside*] Me. You shall not make for yourself any carved image, or any likeness of anything that is in heaven above, or that is in the earth beneath, or that is in the water under the earth; you shall not bow down to them nor serve them. For I, the LORD your God, am a jealous God, visiting the iniquity of the fathers on the children to the third and fourth generations of those who hate Me, but showing mercy to thousands, to those who love Me and keep My commandments."
>
> Exodus 20:3–6

God states specifically that the penalty for involvement with idolatry, false gods and the occult will be visited not merely on the persons guilty, but on the next three generations as well—their sons and daughters, their grandsons and granddaughters, and their great-grandsons and great-granddaughters. You may be in the category of one of these subsequent generations, and there may be a curse over your life because of idolatry or occult practices in previous generations. This is typical of a curse. It goes on from generation to generation until it is dealt with in a scriptural way.

2. Dishonoring Parents

I have dealt with many young people who had a curse over their lives because of a wrong attitude or relationship to their parents. We need to remember Ephesians 6:2–3: "'Honor your father and mother,' which is the first commandment with promise [blessing]: that it may be well with you and you may live long on the earth." Paul meant that this is the first commandment carrying with it a promise of blessing. If you fail to honor your parents, you incur a curse on yourself. If that is your condition, you need to repent, change, adjust your attitude and, if possible, your relationship with your parents. I have never known a person with a wrong attitude to parents who has come under the full blessing of God.

3. Illicit or Unnatural Sex (Adultery, Fornication, Incest, Homosexuality, Bestiality, Etc.)

All these activities bring curses. It is not a matter of whether we wish them to bring curses or whether we think they ought to bring curses. The fact of the matter is, God has so ordered human life that they *do* bring curses.

4. Injustice to the Weak or Helpless

Perhaps the most outstanding example of such injustice is the procurement of abortion—the deliberate killing of unborn children. There can be no greater example of injustice to the weak and helpless than that. If you have been guilty of abortion, there is a curse over your life. I am not saying you cannot escape from the curse, but I am saying you need to recognize the curse, turn to God for mercy and meet His conditions for redemption from the curse.

5. Trusting in Man

Jeremiah states a reason for a curse that most people, even many Christians, have failed to notice. Consequently they have come under the very curse against which they are warned:

> Thus says the LORD:
> "Cursed is the man who trusts in man
> And makes flesh his strength,
> Whose heart departs from the LORD.
> For he shall be like a shrub in the desert,
> And shall not see when good comes,
> But shall inhabit the parched places in the wilderness,
> In a salt land which is not inhabited."
> Jeremiah 17:5–6

The cause stated here is very simple: trusting in man. Remember, *you* are man. Therefore, it is trusting in yourself, making flesh your strength. The result of trusting in man (yourself)—relying on your own natural ability, cleverness or education—is that your heart departs from the Lord, which brings a curse. This also explains why many Christians and churches have lost their blessing. They started in the grace of God with supernatural blessing, anointing and faith, and then went back to trusting human morality, organization or education. None of these things is wrong, but to trust in them brings an individual or church under the curse of God.

Paul dealt with the same theme in Galatians:

> O foolish Galatians! Who has bewitched you that you should not obey the truth, before whose eyes Jesus Christ was clearly portrayed among you as crucified? This only I want to learn from you: Did you receive the Spirit by the works of the law,

or by the hearing of faith? Are you so foolish? Having begun in the Spirit, are you now being made perfect by the flesh?

Galatians 3:1–3

This is the essence of the problem: beginning in the Spirit and God's supernatural grace and ability, and then going back to relying on our own carnal efforts—morality, education, cleverness, programs or finances. If you follow Paul's teaching in that third chapter, you will find that he speaks about the curse and the blessing in verses 13 and 14. You bring yourself under a curse when you go back to legalism, works or seeking to achieve righteousness with God by your own efforts. This is a major problem of countless Christian denominations and organizations. They are under a curse and do not know what they are struggling with, or its cause.

6. Stealing or Perjury

In Zechariah 5:1–4 the prophet had a vision of a flying scroll with a curse on either side of it. The curse on one side was for stealing, the other side for perjury. Zechariah saw the scroll going into people's houses and taking its place there. As a result the houses disintegrated; they just rotted and fell apart. Again, that is typical of what a curse does. It destroys everything around it. Notice, however, the two causes for the curse: stealing and perjury.

7. Being Stingy with God

The prophet Malachi addresses another activity that brings a curse on people:

> "Cursed be the deceiver
> Who has in his flock a male,
> And makes a vow,
> But sacrifices to the Lord what is blemished. . . ."
>
> Malachi 1:14

What is the cause of the curse here? You have promised to give something to God and then draw back on your promise. Being stingy with God brings a curse. Let me urge you, dear friends, do not be stingy with God!

Malachi returns to this theme later:

> "Will a man rob God?
> Yet you have robbed Me!
> But you say,
> 'In what way have we robbed You?'
> In tithes and offerings.
> You are cursed with a curse,
> For you have robbed Me,
> Even this whole nation."
>
> Malachi 3:8–9

What brought a curse on them? Being stingy with God, withholding the offerings due Him. When I see people put miserable sums into church offerings, I just ache for them. They are being stingy with God and bringing a curse on themselves. Let me tell you this very gently: God does not need your tips! If all you are going to put in the offering is a tip, you had better not put in anything.

Then Malachi tells them the remedy:

> "Bring all the tithes into the storehouse,
> That there may be food in My house,
> And prove Me now in this,"
> Says the LORD of hosts,
> "If I will not open for you the windows of heaven
> And pour out for you such blessing
> That there will not be room enough to receive it."
>
> verse 10

The cause for the curse: stinginess with God. The cause for the promised blessing: generosity or liberality with God. Why should we deny ourselves the blessing? Why should we come under the curse of stinginess in our dealings with God when He has freely promised us His blessing if we will just be open and generous with Him?

8. Relational Curses

Another common source of curses proceeds from persons with relational authority. God has ordered human society in such a way that, in certain relationships, one person has authority over another person. A husband, for instance, has authority over his wife; parents have authority over children; teachers have authority over pupils; and pastors have authority over congregations.

Consider Jacob, who lived with his uncle, Laban, for a long time. He acquired two wives (Laban's daughters), two concubines and eleven children. Then, without telling Laban, he fled because he was afraid his uncle would try to hold him back or take his wives from him. His Uncle Laban pursued him in anger.

What Jacob did not know was that his favorite wife, Rachel, had stolen her father's household gods. The Hebrew word is *teraphim*—little idols or images that people would keep in their homes ostensibly to protect them and bring blessing. These were forms of the occult in which Rachel should not have been involved. When Laban caught up with Jacob, he asked him why he had stolen his gods. Jacob, not knowing who had stolen them, declared, "With whomever you find your gods, do not let him live" (Genesis 31:32).

That is a curse. Jacob said it in all innocence. He did not know to whom it applied. But as a husband, he was actually pronouncing a curse on his wife. The next time Rachel gave birth, which was not much later, she died in childbirth. This is cause and effect. It was her husband's curse that caused her death.

Or consider the relational authority of parents. A father may have three sons. The first one, because he is the firstborn, is accepted; the third one, who is talented, is also accepted; but

185

the middle one has nothing special to commend him, so the father does not like him. Maybe he sees too much of himself in this son. In any case the father is always against this middle son. He says, "You'll never succeed. You'll never make good in life. There's no hope for you." That is a curse. I have met many people with natural gifts and talents who could not succeed because they were struggling against a parental curse.

Another example is a teacher saying to her pupil, "You're stupid! You'll never learn to read." Again, that is a curse. I have met people struggling against curses pronounced by teachers decades previously in their lives.

A pastor may say to a member of his congregation, "If you leave this church, you'll never succeed. You'll backslide." What is that? Again, it is a relational curse.

9. Self-Imposed Curses

Curses can also be self-imposed. Rebekah instructed her son Jacob to get the blessing from his father, Isaac. When Jacob feared that Isaac would discover that he was a deceiver and curse him instead of blessing him, Rebekah replied, "Let your curse be on me, my son" (Genesis 27:13). She pronounced a curse on herself.

If you study the story, you find that Rebekah never saw her son Jacob alive again. She was dead by the time he returned. We read that Rebekah began using language like this: "I am weary of my life because of the daughters of Heth . . . what good will my life be to me?" (Genesis 27:46). That language is typical of a person under a curse.

Beware of other sayings like "I wish I were dead" and "What's the good of living?" People who make such comments are pronouncing a curse on themselves. Instead of these, make a positive confession: "I shall not die, but live, and declare the works of the LORD" (Psalm 118:17). Cancel the negative by the positive.

Let's look at one final example of a self-imposed curse that has stained the pages of human history for nineteen centuries. Jesus stood before Pilate, who wanted to release Him. Pilate said, "Shall I let Him go?" The crowds said, "No. Crucify Him!"

Pilate took water, washed his hands in front of the crowd and said, "I am innocent of the blood of this just Person" (Matthew 27:24). The crowd then replied, "His blood be on us and on our children" (verse 25). What is that? A self-imposed curse.

One of the great tragedies of human history is that the Jewish people pronounced a curse on themselves and on their children. I say with the deepest regret that subsequent history illustrates the outworking of that curse. It is still at work today. Oh, thank God that there is provision for release from the curse through the sacrificial death of the Messiah! There is no other way out.

10. Curses from People Representing Satan

Curses may also come from persons who are supernaturally empowered—not by God but by Satan. They have cultivated the evil power of Satan in such a way that they can release it in the lives of others. We call such persons by various names, such as witch doctors, wizards, witches, sorcerers, mediums, clairvoyants, fortune-tellers and false prophets. The Bible clearly states that all who practice such things are detestable to God. Moses said to Israel:

> Let no one be found among you who sacrifices his son or daughter in the fire, who practices divination or sorcery, interprets omens, engages in witchcraft, or casts spells, or who is a medium or spiritist or who consults the dead. Anyone who does these things is detestable to the LORD.
>
> Deuteronomy 18:10–12, NIV

Notice the list of activities: divination (which is fortune-telling); sorcery; interpreting omens (that would include teacup reading); engaging in witchcraft; casting spells; being a medium; being a spiritist; consulting the dead. "Anyone who does these things is detestable to the LORD." Furthermore, those who resort to such persons expose themselves to satanic influence.

The Bible describes such a person, whom we would refer to as a "witch doctor."

The Israelites had arrived at the land of their inheritance and were camped on the borders of the territory of Moab. Balak, king of Moab, was extremely frightened. He knew he could not defeat these people in war, so he resorted to a practice typical in the Middle East today and in various other nations. He called for the witch doctor, or sorcerer, whose name was Balaam. He asked Balaam to curse this people:

> "Look, a people has come from Egypt. See, they cover the face of the earth, and are settling next to me! Therefore please come at once, curse this people for me, for they are too mighty for me. Perhaps I shall be able to defeat them and drive them out of the land, for I know that he whom you bless is blessed, and he whom you curse is cursed."
>
> Numbers 22:5–6

This is typical practice among primitive tribes in Africa, even today. If they go out to war against one another, they do not go straight to battle. First they get the witch doctor to pronounce a curse on the opposing tribe, because once that tribe is under a curse, they believe they will be able to defeat it.

Some people regard this as empty superstition. God did not regard it that way. On the contrary, He took Balak's offer very seriously and intervened sovereignly to prevent Balaam from cursing Israel. Moses told Israel later:

> "[The Moabites] hired against you Balaam the son of Beor from Pethor of Mesopotamia, to curse you. Nevertheless the LORD your God would not listen to Balaam, but the LORD your God turned the curse into a blessing for you, because the LORD your God loves you."
>
> Deuteronomy 23:4–5

God took it so seriously that He stood against Balaam and, in Moses' words, "turned the curse into a blessing." The Bible never says Satan has no power. It is a mistake to believe that. The Bible clearly teaches that Satan has supernatural power. But Jesus promised His disciples superior power:

> "Behold, I give you the authority to trample on serpents and scorpions, and over all the power of the enemy, and nothing shall by any means hurt you."
>
> Luke 10:19

Rather than believe Satan is powerless, take refuge in the glorious fact that Jesus has given His disciples power over all the power of Satan.

I want to illustrate this reality by three examples from personal experience.

For five years I was principal of a teacher training college in East Africa. One of my students from a remote village told me that, in his village, two families had quarreled and become bitter against one another. One family sent for the local witch doctor, gave him a goat as payment and said, "Put a curse on the other family." The witch doctor agreed. He took the goat, went away and put a curse on the other family's little son. At midnight on a certain day, he told his client family, a jackal would cry in the village, at which point the son of that family would die. It happened exactly that way. A jackal cried and the son died. It was the outworking of a curse. Curses have power.

Another incident I remember concerns the pastor of a church. In order to raise funds, some of the church members organized what they called a "garden fete." They had all sorts of entertainments and attractions to amuse people, including a fortune-teller, whom they regarded simply as a joke. The pastor was not too happy about it, but he agreed. He went into the tent to have his fortune told. The fortune-teller told him his wife would get cancer. The pastor told me afterward that his blood ran cold and his heart almost stopped beating. He had unwittingly exposed himself to a curse from a servant of Satan that affected his wife.

Do you know what happened? His wife did get cancer. But through prayer, faith and the help of doctors, she was ultimately healed. Praise God!

Here is a final experience. In Chicago many years back, while I was pastoring a church, a woman told me that she had been a spiritist medium but that she wanted deliverance. I was somewhat skeptical, but began to pray with her to drive out the power of Satan from her life. It was hard going, and in the middle I stopped to rest for a few moments. Suddenly she looked at me and said, "I see you in a car and it's wrecked against a tree." I realized that Satan's destiny for my life was being pronounced through the lips of that woman. Thank God I was on the alert. "I'll never be in any car that will be wrecked against a tree," I declared. "I reject that curse. It has no power over me." But if I had said, "Oh, no! I'm going to be in a car and it's going to be wrecked against a tree," I would have accepted that curse and it would have been worked out in my life.

11. Curses from Soulish Prayers, Utterances and Gossip

Another cause of curses is soulish prayers, utterances and gossip:

> If you have bitter envy and self-seeking in your hearts, do not boast and lie against the truth. This wisdom does not descend from above, but is earthly, sensual, demonic.
>
> James 3:14–15

People can talk and even pray against one another. In so doing, if they are not in the realm of the Spirit but in the realm of the soul, they pray from bad or evil emotions, and the effect of their prayer is a curse.

I was in a church in which a group of people was actually praying for the death of the pastor's wife. That was a curse! It was the result of bitterness, hatred and division in the church.

In Jeremiah's day here is what the people who opposed him said:

"Come and let us devise plans against Jeremiah. . . . Come on and let us strike at him with our tongue, and let us give no heed to any of his words."

Jeremiah 18:18, NASB

Do you realize how we can wound people with our tongues, instead of blessing them? Many servants of God have been sliced by tongues of gossip, soulish utterances and prayers.

12. Curses from Unscriptural Covenants

Finally, curses may come from unscriptural covenants by which people commit themselves to other people committed to false gods. God said through Moses to Israel, regarding the idolatrous inhabitants of the land, "You shall make no covenant with them, nor with their gods" (Exodus 23:32). If you make a covenant with people who are in false religions and worshiping false gods, not only do you make a covenant with the people, but you also make a covenant with their gods.

Let me give you one example, which I present with care. Freemasonry is a secret society that can bring terrible curses on the people involved in it. I have seen this worked out in the lives of family members through retarded children, paralyzed children, broken homes and other symptoms of curses. Anyone involved in Freemasonry should look diligently for symptoms of curses in their lives and follow the steps I will enumerate in the next chapter.

twenty-nine

How to Pass from Curse to Blessing

BEFORE I BEGIN to explain in specific, practical terms how you may pass from curse to blessing, let me review some of the main points.

These are the common indications that there may be a curse over your life:

1. Mental or emotional breakdown.
2. Repeated or chronic sicknesses, especially if these are hereditary or without clear medical diagnosis.
3. Repeated miscarriages or related female problems or barrenness.
4. Breakdown of marriage, or family alienation in general.
5. Continuing financial insufficiency, especially where the income appears sufficient.
6. Being accident-prone.
7. History of suicides or unnatural deaths in the family.

There are also a number of common causes of curses. Remember what the Bible says: A curse does not come without a cause. In the last chapter I listed twelve possible sources:

1. Foremost are idolatry, false gods and the occult.
2. Dishonoring parents.
3. Illicit or unnatural sex.
4. Injustice to the weak or helpless. The supreme example of that in our society is intentional abortion.
5. Trusting in the arm of flesh.
6. Stealing or perjury.
7. Financial stinginess with God.
8. Words spoken by persons with relational authority, such as parents, husbands, teachers or pastors.
9. Self-imposed curses—curses that people pronounce on themselves.
10. Words pronounced by persons representing Satan— witch doctors, etc.
11. Soulish prayers and utterances spoken in wrong attitudes, and gossip.
12. Unscriptural covenants—being united by covenant with people united with forces that are evil and alien to God (for example, Freemasonry).

In practical terms, how can we pass from curse to blessing? The basis of all deliverance from a curse is the sacrificial atonement of Jesus. Once again, Galatians 3:13–14:

> Christ has redeemed us from the curse of the law, having become a curse for us (for it is written, "Cursed is everyone who hangs on a tree"), that the blessing of Abraham might come upon the Gentiles in Christ Jesus. . . .

The transition from curse to blessing is made possible because, on the cross, Jesus was made a curse with the curse due to us that we might in return receive the blessing due to His sinless obedience. This is stated generally in Isaiah 53:6:

> All we like sheep have gone astray;
> We have turned, every one, to his own way;
> And the LORD has laid on Him the iniquity of us all.

The word *iniquity*, by way of review, means not only rebellion but all the evil consequences of rebellion. One of those evil consequences is the curse that comes from not hearing and obeying God's voice.

The Primary Requirement

Once you have met the conditions and claimed your deliverance, I want to remind you very emphatically that thereafter God still requires obedience. Recall the words of Moses:

> It shall come to pass, if you diligently obey the voice of the LORD your God, to observe carefully all His commandments which I command you today, that the LORD your God will set you high above all nations of the earth. And all these blessings shall come upon you and overtake you, because you obey the voice of the LORD your God.
>
> Deuteronomy 28:1–2

Once we have been delivered from the curse and entered into the blessing, we must meet these simple, basic conditions to remain in the blessing. We must listen carefully to God's voice and do what He says. These are ongoing conditions. If we again turn away and refuse to hear and obey God's voice, we expose ourselves automatically once again to the curse.

This requirement was given not just for keeping clear of curses. It is the universal requirement for enjoying God's favor—having the light of His countenance on us and living in His salvation, blessing and provision. Jesus said the same in simple language for all who want to follow and serve Him as Christian disciples: "My sheep hear My voice, and I know them, and they follow Me" (John 10:27).

What is the basic requirement for being a Christian? It does not have to do with the church you attend or your denominational label. Those things are secondary. The primary requirement is hearing the voice of Jesus and following Him. This runs all through the Bible: "If you diligently heed the voice of the LORD your God and do what is right in His sight . . ." (Exodus 15:26). "The sheep hear his voice; and he calls his own sheep by name and leads them out" (John 10:3). You cannot escape that basic requirement.

You can come out from under a curse and commit yourself to the grace of God. Thereafter you are responsible to live your life in such a way that you continue in the grace and blessings of God.

In order to come out from under the curse and into the blessing, we have to move from what I call the "legal" to the "experiential." Jesus has already made the provision; that happened more than nineteen centuries ago. On the cross He was made a curse so that we might receive the blessing. That is already provided. But we must make it real in our personal experience.

This is true of every aspect of Jesus' work on the cross. He was punished that we might be forgiven. He was wounded that we might be healed. All that has been done. In order to receive forgiveness, however, we must do what God requires. In order to be healed, we must do what God commands. We must *appropriate* this provision in our own personal lives, passing from the legal to the experiential.

To do this in the case of curses, we often need to discover the cause or source of the curse. That is why I have taken so much space to deal with the various possible causes or sources of curses.

Four Steps to Take

Once we have identified the cause or source in experience where we—or, in many cases, our ancestors or others associated

195

with us—were exposed to the curse, there are four things we must do: *recognize, repent, renounce, resist.*

1. *Recognize:* We must recognize the true nature of our problem and, if possible, the source or cause of the curse—that is, the sin or problem through which it originally entered.
2. *Repent:* We must repent of whatever exposed us to the problem, whether our own sin or the sin of our ancestors.
3. *Renounce:* We must say, "It no longer belongs to me. I do not accept it. Through Jesus I have the right to be free from it. It's not my problem any longer."
4. *Resist:* We must take a definite, active stand against the power of Satan.

Resisting the devil is one of the things the Bible tells us we must do: "Submit to God. Resist the devil and he will flee from you" (James 4:7). Notice the order. What is the first thing we must do? Submit to God. Once we have submitted to God, we can resist the devil, and the Bible says he will flee from us.

Once you have taken these four steps—recognize, repent, renounce, resist—you are ready to come to God and to claim your release by a very specific prayer.

thirty

THE PROCESS OF RELEASE

ONCE YOU HAVE TAKEN the four steps I enumerated in the last chapter, there are seven requirements your prayer of release needs to fulfill in order to be thoroughly in line with God and what He expects of you. I will state these requirements in order.

1. Base Your Faith on God's Word

First, your faith must be based on God's Word. I will give you some very powerful Scriptures that will provide you with this basis in God's Word. First, once again:

Christ has redeemed us from the curse of the law, having become a curse for us (for it is written, "Cursed is everyone who hangs on a tree"), that the blessing of Abraham might come upon the Gentiles in Christ Jesus. . . .

Galatians 3:13–14

Christ was made a curse on the cross, and by that He has redeemed us. He has bought us back from the curse that we might receive the blessing.

In Him we have redemption through His blood, the forgiveness of sins, according to the riches of His grace.

Ephesians 1:7

Redemption comes through the blood of Jesus. Through the blood of Jesus we can have our sins forgiven, be bought back out of the hand of the devil and redeemed from the curse.

[God] rescued us from the domain of darkness, and transferred us to the kingdom of His beloved Son, in whom we have redemption, the forgiveness of sins.

Colossians 1:13–14, NASB

Through our faith in Jesus and His sacrificial death, God has delivered us from the domain of darkness. Notice that word *domain*. In the original Greek it is *authority*. Satan has authority over the disobedient, unbelieving and unsaved. But through Jesus God has delivered us from that domain of darkness and transferred us into the Kingdom of the Son of His love, in whom we have redemption. Now note that key word *redemption*. We have been bought back. We are no longer under the power of the curse because of the redeeming death and shed blood of Jesus Christ.

For this purpose the Son of God was manifested, that He might destroy the works of the devil.

1 John 3:8

Why did Jesus come? To destroy the works of the devil. That includes the curse!

198

"Behold, I give you the authority to trample on serpents and scorpions, and over all the power of the enemy, and nothing shall by any means hurt you."

Luke 10:19

Satan has power, but Jesus has given us power over the power of Satan, so "nothing shall by any means hurt [us]."

2. Confess Your Faith

Once you have based your faith on those Scriptures and grasped them as realities for yourself, the second requirement is confessing your faith in Christ. Hebrews 3:1 says that Jesus is the "High Priest of our confession." It is the confession of our faith in Jesus that releases Him to operate as our High Priest in the supernatural realm. If we do not make a confession, we do not release Him to operate on our behalf. But when we make the right confession, then He serves as our High Priest.

3. Commit to Obeying God

The third requirement is to commit yourself to obedience. The blessings come to those who hear and obey the voice of God. In order to remain free from the curse once you are released, you must commit yourself to hearing and obeying the voice of God. You cannot rely on your own efforts or righteousness to fulfill this commitment. When you make this commitment in faith, you release the grace of God in your life. This enables you to do what you have committed yourself to do in faith.

4. Confess

Fourth, you must confess any known sins that either you or your ancestors have committed. Why your ancestors? Because, as we have seen, it may be that the sin of your ancestors exposed you, as one of their descendants, to the curse. You do not bear the guilt of their sin, but you do suffer the consequences. In order to escape from the curse, you need to deal with the sin that exposed you or your ancestors to the curse. You do that by confessing and asking God to forgive and blot out that sin.

> He who covers his sins will not prosper,
> But whoever confesses and forsakes them will have mercy.
> Proverbs 28:13

If you cover sin, you will not prosper or be blessed. But if you confess and forsake sin, then you will find God's mercy and redemption from the curse.

5. Forgive

The fifth requirement is to forgive all other persons. Jesus said, "Whenever you stand praying, forgive, if you have anything against anyone, so that your Father who is in heaven will also forgive you your transgressions" (Mark 11:25, NASB).

This is very important. Jesus makes it clear that if we hold unforgiveness, bitterness or resentment in our hearts when we pray, it will be a barrier to the answer to our prayer. It will keep us under the curse. By a decision of our will, when we pray, we must lay down any resentment, bitterness or unforgiveness against any person. In the measure in which we forgive others, God forgives us. If we want total forgiveness from God, we must offer total forgiveness to others. This is not being super-spiritual; forgiving others is what I call "enlightened self-interest"!

6. Renounce the Occult

Sixth, you must renounce all contact with the occult or secret societies, by yourself or your ancestors, for the reason

I have already stated. Get rid of all contact objects—anything associated in any way with the occult—and destroy them. This is what Moses said to Israel:

> "You shall burn the carved images of their gods with fire; you shall not covet the silver or gold that is on them, nor take it for yourselves, lest you be snared by it; for it is an abomination to the LORD your God. Nor shall you bring an abomination into your house, lest you be doomed to destruction like it. You shall utterly detest it and utterly abhor it, for it is an accursed thing."
>
> Deuteronomy 7:25–26

Your bringing any accursed object into your house brings the curse on you. You cannot expect deliverance from the curse if you keep any kind of accursed item in your home. Any idol, image, charm or representation of superstition (like a horseshoe upside down)—all these can cause a curse. You must get rid of them if you want to be released from the curse.

7. Release Yourself

The seventh requirement is to release yourself in the name of Jesus. Let me give you two Scriptures:

> It shall come to pass, that whosoever shall call on the name of the LORD shall be delivered. . . .
>
> Joel 2:32, KJV

If you call on the name of the Lord Jesus Christ, you will be delivered. Make sure of that!

Then, Jesus said:

> "Assuredly, I say to you, whatever you bind on earth will be bound in heaven, and whatever you loose on earth will be loosed in heaven."
>
> Matthew 18:18

201

This gives you authority, when you meet the conditions, to loose *yourself* on earth. When you do it on earth, you are loosed in heaven.

Summary

Let me list these seven requirements, in order:

1. Your whole operation must be based on faith in God's Word.
2. You must confess your faith in Christ.
3. You must commit yourself to obedience.
4. You must confess any known sins of yourself or your ancestors.
5. You must forgive all other persons.
6. You must renounce all contact with the occult or secret societies and get rid of all contact objects.
7. You may then release yourself in the name of Jesus from the curse.

If your prayer covers all these points, you can have the assurance that you have fulfilled God's requirements, and you can trust in God's mercy, faithfulness and power.

thirty-one

THE PRAYER OF RELEASE

I AM GOING TO GIVE you the prayer of release. It is important that you read through it once before you pray it, so that you have an intelligent understanding of what you will be doing and saying. Also, by reading it first you will be able to think it over and decide in your heart if you want to say the prayer. You need to be sure you want to say the prayer, because to do so you will be required to make a commitment.

Here is the prayer:

Lord Jesus Christ,

I believe that You are the Son of God and the only way to God; that on the cross You died for my sins; that You rose again from the dead; and that on the cross You were made a curse, so that I might be redeemed from the curse and receive Your blessing.

I trust You now for mercy and forgiveness, and I commit myself from now on, by Your grace, to follow and obey You.

I ask You to forgive and blot out any sins committed by me or by my ancestors that exposed me to a curse. [At this point, name any specific sins of which you are aware.]

If people have harmed me or wronged me, I forgive them, as I would have God forgive me. [Name these people.]

I renounce all contact with Satan, occult practices and unscriptural secret societies. If I have any contact objects that link me to these things, I promise to destroy them. [Name the specific practices and/or secret societies with which you were involved.]

With the authority You have given me as a child of God, I release myself from every curse that has ever come upon me or affected me in any way.

In the name of Jesus. Amen.

Notice that at certain points in the prayer, you are to name any *specific* practices, sins or persons known to you. It is important, if possible, to be specific about these things when dealing with God.

Now that you have read the prayer through once, take a few minutes to decide whether you want to commit yourself.

Turn your heart and mind toward the Lord Jesus and focus on Him. When you pray the prayer, say it out loud.

Jesus has heard your prayer. Receive your release by faith, immediately. The simplest way to do this is to begin to thank God. Thanksgiving is the simplest and purest expression of faith. Accept your release as an accomplished fact. If you undergo any kind of strange emotional or physical reaction, do not let it frighten you. It is a good sign. It means God is moving to release you, even emotionally or physically. It is important to keep thanking Him.

I, as the Lord's servant, pray this prayer for each of you who have claimed your release:

O God, I thank You that You allowed Jesus, on the cross, to become a curse, that we, through faith in Him, might be redeemed from the curse. I thank You for everyone who has prayed this prayer in faith, meeting Your conditions. Lord Jesus, I claim their release for them now, as they are thanking You. I claim a full release. I break every satanic power over these lives. I revoke every curse. I declare that Satan is a defeated enemy, that all his claims have been canceled by the shed blood of Jesus. I pronounce them free in the name of Jesus. I declare that Satan's authority is revoked and canceled forever. In the name of Jesus. Amen.

Appendix 1

By This I Overcome the Devil

I TESTIFY to Satan personally as to what the Word of God says the blood of Jesus does for me:

Through the blood of Jesus, I am redeemed out of the hand of the devil.

Through the blood of Jesus, all my sins are forgiven.

The blood of Jesus Christ, God's Son, continually cleanses me from all sin.

Through the blood of Jesus, I am justified, made righteous, *just-as-if-I'd* never sinned.

Through the blood of Jesus, I am sanctified, made holy, set apart to God.

My body is a temple of the Holy Spirit, redeemed and cleansed by the blood of Jesus.

Satan has no place in me, no power over me, through the blood of Jesus.

Based on the following Scriptures (all in the NKJV):

Revelation 12:11: "They overcame him by the blood of the Lamb [Jesus Christ] and by the word of their testimony [that is, they testified to what the Word of God says about the blood of Jesus], and they did not love their lives to the death."

Ephesians 1:7: "In Him we have redemption through His blood, the forgiveness of sins, according to the riches of His grace."

Psalm 107:2: "Let the redeemed of the LORD say so, whom He has redeemed from the hand of the enemy."

1 John 1:7: "If we walk in the light as He is in the light, we have fellowship with one another, and the blood of Jesus Christ His Son cleanses us from all sin."

Romans 5:9: "Much more then, having now been justified by His blood, we shall be saved from wrath through Him."

Hebrews 13:12: "Jesus also, that He might sanctify the people with His own blood, suffered outside the gate."

1 Corinthians 6:19–20: "Do you not know that your body is the temple of the Holy Spirit who is in you, whom you have from God, and you are not your own? For you were bought at a price; therefore glorify God in your body and in your spirit, which are God's."

Appendix 2

CONFESSION FOR OVERCOMERS

MY BODY IS A TEMPLE for the Holy Spirit, redeemed, cleansed and sanctified by the blood of Jesus. My members—the parts of my body—are instruments of righteousness, yielded to God for His service and for His glory. The devil has no place in me, no power over me, no unsettled claims against me. All has been settled by the blood of Jesus. I overcome Satan by the blood of the Lamb and by the word of my testimony, and I love not my life unto the death. My body is for the Lord and the Lord is for my body. Amen.

Based on the following Scriptures (all in the NKJV):

1 Corinthians 6:19–20: "Do you not know that your body is the temple of the Holy Spirit who is in you, whom you have from God, and you are not your own? For you were bought at a price; therefore glorify God in your body and in your spirit, which are God's."

Ephesians 1:7: "In Him we have redemption through His blood, the forgiveness of sins, according to the riches of His grace."

Psalm 107:2: "Let the redeemed of the LORD say so, whom He has redeemed from the hand of the enemy."

1 John 1:7: "If we walk in the light as He is in the light, we have fellowship with one another, and the blood of Jesus Christ His Son cleanses us from all sin."

Hebrews 13:12: "Jesus also, that He might sanctify the people with His own blood, suffered outside the gate."

Romans 6:13: "Do not present your members as instruments of unrighteousness to sin, but present yourselves to God as being alive from the dead, and your members as instruments of righteousness to God."

Romans 8:33–34: "Who shall bring a charge against God's elect? It is God who justifies. Who is he who condemns? It is Christ who died, and furthermore is also risen, who is even at the right hand of God, who also makes intercession for us."

Revelation 12:11: "They overcame him by the blood of the Lamb [Jesus Christ] and by the word of their testimony [that is, they testified to what the Word of God says about the blood of Jesus], and they did not love their lives to the death."

1 Corinthians 6:13: "Foods for the stomach and the stomach for foods, but God will destroy both it and them. Now the body is not for sexual immorality but for the Lord, and the Lord for the body."

Appendix 3

DECLARATION OF CONFIDENCE IN GOD'S PROTECTION

SOMEONE ASKED my second wife, Ruth, and me, "How do you protect yourself if you live in the Middle East or someplace where people put curses on other people?"

There are many answers I could give, but here is just one thing Ruth and I did to protect ourselves on a daily basis. We made a nighttime proclamation based on the following Scripture:

> "No weapon formed against you shall prosper, and every tongue which rises against you in judgment you shall condemn. This is the heritage of the servants of the LORD, and their righteousness is from Me," says the LORD.
>
> Isaiah 54:17, NKJV

The important statement is *Our righteousness is from the Lord.* If we were to come against Satan in our own righteousness, we would have nothing to stand on! But the Lord has covered us with a robe of His righteousness.

Every night Ruth and I made this declaration, the last thing before we went to sleep:

No weapon that is formed against us shall prosper, and every tongue that rises against us in judgment we do condemn. This is our heritage as servants of the Lord, and our righteousness is from You, O Lord of hosts. If there are those who have been speaking or praying against us, or seeking harm or evil for us, or who have rejected us, we forgive them and, having forgiven them, we bless them in the name of the Lord.

Now we declare, O Lord, that You and You alone are our God, and besides You there is no other—a just God and Savior, the Father, the Son and the Spirit—and we worship You.

We submit ourselves afresh to you tonight in unreserved obedience. Having submitted to You, Lord, we do as Your Word directs. We resist the devil—all his pressures, his attacks, his deceptions, every instrument or agent he would seek to use against us. We do not submit! We resist him, drive him from us and exclude him from us in the name of Jesus. Specifically, we reject and repel:

Infirmity
Pain
Infection
Inflammation
Malignancies
Allergies
Viruses
Every form of witchcraft

Finally, Lord, we thank You that through the sacrifice of Jesus on the cross, we have passed out from under the curse and entered into the blessing of Abraham whom You blessed in all things:

Exaltation
Health

Reproductiveness
Prosperity
Victory
God's favor

Amen.

[See Matthew 5:43; Romans 12:14; Galatians 3:13–14; Genesis 24:1.]

Appendix 4

PROCLAMATIONS
ON BEHALF OF ISRAEL

Jeremiah 31:10: "He who scattered Israel will gather [or is gathering] him, and keep him as a shepherd does his flock" (NKJV).

Psalm 129:5–6: "Let them all be confounded and turned back that hate Zion. Let them be as the grass upon the housetops, which withereth afore it groweth up" (KJV).

Psalm 55:9: "Destroy, O Lord, and divide their tongues . . ." (NKJV).

Psalm 125:3: "The scepter of the wicked will not remain over the land allotted to the righteous . . ." (NIV).

1 Samuel 12:22: "The LORD will not forsake His people, for His great name's sake, because it has pleased the LORD to make you [or Israel] His people" (NKJV).

Psalm 33:8–12: "Let all the earth fear the LORD; let all the inhabitants of the world stand in awe of Him. For He spoke, and it was done; He commanded, and it stood fast. The LORD brings the counsel of the nations to nothing; He makes the plans of the peoples of no effect. The counsel of the LORD stands forever, the plans of His heart to all generations. Blessed is the nation whose God is the LORD, and the people whom He has chosen as His own inheritance" (NKJV).

Psalm 17:7–9: "Show Your marvelous lovingkindness by Your right hand, O You who save those who trust in You from those who rise up against them. Keep me [or *Israel*] as the apple of Your eye; hide [her] under the shadow of Your wings, from the wicked who oppress [her], from [her] deadly enemies who surround [her]" (NKJV).

Psalm 124:1–8: "'If it had not been the LORD who was on our side,' let Israel now say—'If it had not been the LORD who was on our side, when men rose up against us, then they would have swallowed us alive, when their wrath was kindled against us; then the waters would have overwhelmed us, the stream would have gone over our soul; then the swollen waters would have gone over our soul.' Blessed be the LORD, who has not given us as prey to their teeth. Our soul has escaped as a bird from the snare of the fowlers; the snare is broken, and we have escaped. Our help is in the name of the LORD, who made heaven and earth" (NKJV).

Subject Index

SCRIPTURE INDEX

222

223

Derek Prince (1915–2003) was born in India of British parents. Educated as a scholar of Greek and Latin at Eton College and Cambridge University, England, he held a fellowship in ancient and modern philosophy at King's College. He also studied several modern languages, including Hebrew and Aramaic, at Cambridge University and the Hebrew University in Jerusalem.

While serving with the British army in World War II, he began to study the Bible and experienced a life-changing encounter with Jesus Christ. Out of this encounter he formed two conclusions: first, that Jesus Christ is alive; second, that the Bible is a true, relevant, up-to-date book. These conclusions altered the whole course of his life, which he then devoted to studying and teaching the Bible.

Derek's main gift of explaining the Bible and its teaching in a clear and simple way has helped build a foundation of faith in millions of lives. His nondenominational, nonsectarian approach has made his teaching equally relevant and helpful to people from all racial and religious backgrounds.

He is the author of over fifty books and five hundred audio and one hundred sixty video teaching cassettes, many of which have been translated and published in more than sixty languages. His daily radio broadcast, *Keys to Successful Living*, is translated into Arabic, Chinese (Amoy, Cantonese, Mandarin, Shanghaiese, Swatow), Croatian, German, Malagasy, Mongolian, Russian, Samoan, Spanish and Tongan. His daily radio program continues to touch lives around the world.

For more information, please call or write:

Derek Prince Ministries
P.O. Box 19501
Charlotte, NC 28219-9501
USA
(704) 357-3556
www.dpmusa.org